THE TOTALLY AWESOME BOOK OF CRAZY STORIES

Crazy But True Stories
That Actually Happened!

BILL O'NEILL

ISBN: 978-1-64845-070-9

DON'T FORGET YOUR FREE BOOKS

CONTENTS

INTRODUCTION

When you learn about topics like history, Shakespeare, science, and politics at high school, the problem is that quite often some of the weirdest and most interesting stories are left out of the textbooks and exam papers.

So you end up analyzing sonnets and monologues, instead of finding out that Shakespeare's father was the official beer taster of Stratford upon Avon. You end up learning about the early diplomatic policies of the fledgling United States, rather than learning the story of how President John Quincy Adams once almost drowned while trying to swim across the Potomac River naked during a thunderstorm. Plus, you end up studying the Ancient Egyptians, without ever being told that Ramses III had to deal with the first labor strike in recorded history, or that pharaohs had to run around the grounds of the palaces every three years to prove how youthful and fit to rule they still were.

Thankfully, it's precisely these kinds of stories that this book reveals. What follows are some of the craziest, weirdest, funniest, wackiest, and most awesome stories that you'll have hopefully never heard before.

In this story, you'll find out what happened when an ill-fated, ragtag band of French soldiers attempted to invade Britain in the middle of winter. Here too is the story of what happened when Scotland tried to establish a colony in Central America, by landing their ships in the middle of a fetid swamp. Most interesting - is the tale of the man who won an international French Scrabble competition, without being able to speak a single word of French. Plus did you know that the football World Cup trophy was once found by a dog, stuffed under a hedge in a plastic shopping bag? Or that the Prussian King Frederick the Great once tried to dissuade his subjects from drinking coffee in the morning, and instead tried to get them to drink beer? Plus, did you know that when an outbreak of the plague struck the city of London in the mid-17th century that doctors' recommended people protect themselves by sniffing a jar containing their farts? (If you want to know why, don't worry, that story is in here too…)

So without further ado, let's get started.

CHAPTER 1

THE MUMMY WHO NEEDED A PASSPORT

From working out the movements of the stars to building geometrically and architecturally-perfect pyramids, the Ancient Egyptians were certainly proficient at a great many things. But as advanced as their civilization was, unfortunately, they weren't quite up-to-date enough to begin issuing passports to their citizens - and in the mid-1970s, that posed something of a problem...

The mummified remains of one of Egypt's greatest pharaohs, Ramses II, were discovered in 1881 alongside the bodies of more than 50 Egyptian noblemen, high priests, and rulers. They were found in a secret chamber at an ancient royal burial complex known as Deir el-Bahri, on the west bank of the river Nile. Pharaoh Ramses—who ruled over his kingdom for more than six decades, from 1,279-1,213 BCE—had originally been buried in Ancient Egypt's famous Valley of the Kings, but so great was his power and influence at the time of his death that those who went on to succeed him feared that his tomb may be the target of looters and grave robbers. As a result, his priests and advisors later had his remains removed to a more distant location, in an ancient Theban burial cache or "necropolis," Deir el-Bahri, opposite the grand city of Luxor.

There, Ramses remained undisturbed for the next three millennia, until a team of archeologists discovered his remains in the late 19th century.

After the discovery, it was decided that Ramses' remains be put on display - alongside many of his treasures and burial trappings - as the centerpiece of a grand new exhibition at the national Egyptian Museum in Cairo. After more than 90 years on display to the public, however, in 1974 archeologists in Cairo realized that Ramses' mummified body was beginning to deteriorate and break down at an alarming rate. Fearing that the mummy might eventually disintegrate altogether, arrangements were quickly made for it to be shipped to a team of expert archeological restorers in Paris, France, for examination where it was hoped, that expert treatment and some much-needed repair would occur.

There was, however, a problem. Customs and travel laws between Egypt and Europe in the 1970s demanded that everyone wishing to travel between the two places needed to have valid documentation. And what is more, those laws were so stringent that they even applied to dead bodies!

As a result, some 3,189 years after his death, Pharaoh Ramses II was issued with an official Egyptian passport, complete with a headshot photograph, and some brief identification details. The pharaoh's occupation, just for the record, was listed as "KING (DECEASED)."

In the typically majestic style, as befits a king, on his arrival in France in September 1976, Ramses' mummy was greeted at

4

the Le Bourget Airport in Paris with full military honors and was then transported to a high-tech laboratory at the city's Musée de l'Homme under an impressive police escort. It was there that his remains were assessed and given a special irradiating anti-fungal treatment to prevent any further deterioration. Given that the chance to carry out such in-depth analysis on a three millennium-old corpse doesn't come along too often, the museum also took the opportunity to carry out a full forensic examination of his remains, under the watchful eye of Pierre-Fernand Ceccaldi, the chief professor of forensic science at Paris' Criminal Identification Laboratory of Paris.

Professor Ceccaldi's examination revealed that the ancient king had suffered several battle wounds and had broken several bones in his life; had likely also suffered from both arthritis and poor circulation; and, astonishingly, he was even able to tell that Pharaoh Ramses—like many of the members of his dynastic line—likely had wavy or curly ginger-colored hair.

With the examination and preservation treatment over, Ramses' mummy was once more prepared for travel. (The official paperwork Ramses had been issued with allowed not only for his mummy to be safely shipped to France but also ensured that it could be returned safely and without any unnecessary hold-up.) Ultimately, in May 1977, he was successfully returned to Cairo and has remained on display in the city's Egyptian Museum ever since.

CHAPTER 2

WHAT EXACTLY IS "TIME IMMEMORIAL"?

You will likely have heard people say that something has taken place "since time immemorial." It's such a familiar phrase that it's almost become a cliché—used to describe anything particularly ancient, well-established, aged, or longstanding.

The word *immemorial* itself essentially means "unrememberable," or literally "beyond all memory." The term *time immemorial*, ultimately, describes any period beyond that which can easily or accurately be recalled by people alive today. But that fairly imprecise definition isn't the only definition of this curious phrase recorded in the dictionary. In fact—in legal contexts in particular—the expression *time immemorial* quite literally, and very specifically, refers to any time before July 6, 1189.

So why does such a specific meaning exist? And where on earth does it come from?

In legal contexts, the concept of *time immemorial* was originally introduced to British statute law, during the reign of King Edward I in the late 13th century. King Edward oversaw the introduction of three influential directives collectively known as the Statutes of Westminster. This was a trio of formal legal documents that attempted to codify all the laws of England, and thereby establish a new and fully comprehensive English legal system in writing for the very first time. (Ironically, despite establishing the foundations of much of the legal system that still survives in England today, all three of these documents were originally written in French!)

The first of these Statutes was compiled in 1275 and defined all manner of important legal concepts like slander, electoral freedom, and 'Acts of God'. And Clause 39 of this first Statute, - officially titled "The Limitation of Prescription Act"; sought to define a standardized cut-off point for assessments of legal ownership.

"No one is to be given a hearing to claim seisin," the document stated, "by any ancestor of his further back than the time of King Richard, uncle of King Henry, the father of the present king." (Seisin being an old name for feudal ownership of land.)

In other words, Clause 39 of the First Statute of Westminster implied that if you ever had your ownership of a given property or plot of land legally challenged, all you had to do to quash the challenge was prove that you and your ancestors had maintained ownership of that property since before King Richard I, (Edward I's great uncle) had ascended to the throne. King Richard's ascendancy took place on 6 July, 1189, and ultimately, it was this date that was established as the legal cut-off point for living memory. Anything that occurred before that date was therefore deemed to be beyond living memory—or, in legal parlance at least, *'time immemorial'*.

Incredibly, this definition remained in force in England right through to 1832, when it was finally decided that being legally compelled to demonstrate personal ownership of something for 643 years could prove somewhat difficult! As a result, in 1832 the King of England, William IV (the uncle of Queen Victoria, who succeeded him five years later), passed the so-called Prescription Act, which shortened the legally required length of ownership for use of a contested property to anything from 20 to 60 years, depending on the type of property in question.

As for *'time immemorial'*, it came to be used more loosely as an expression over time, becoming just another word for an inexpressibly long duration. But its original meaning — thanks to some obscure legal jargon, and a little bit of help from King Richard I; was originally a great deal more specific than that.

CHAPTER 3

A CALL TO PRAYER

Uprisings and rebellions have been sparked by all kinds of different grievances over the centuries—but among the most peculiar has to be a short-lived rebellion in the far southwest corner of Tudor England, which was essentially sparked by nothing more than the publication of a prayer book.

The seeds of this particular rebellion were sown during the reign of the infamous English King Henry VIII. Henry's desire to father a male heir to succeed him and maintain the Tudor name famously led to his increasingly bloody string of marriages and consorts. But not only that, by the time he did secure a male successor—who eventually ascended to the throne as Edward VI, Henry's behavior had seen him fall foul of the Pope, sever England's ties to the Catholic Church, ransack England's monasteries and claim their treasures as his own, and in the process, he stoked violent pockets of resentment and unrest all across his kingdom.

Worsening the situation, when Henry died in 1547, his heir, Edward, was just 9 years old and was already in very poor health himself. As a result, the increasingly disgruntled population of England found themselves ruled not by a powerful and unifying new king, but by a regency panel of warring advisors and clerks, who were left to take decisions on Edward's behalf.

As if this absence of a new national figurehead wasn't bad enough for the English people, the fallout from Henry's departure from the Catholic Church continued to have repercussions in the early years of King Edward's reign. In 1549, Edward's advisors decided that the newly-emerging Church of England, with the English monarch now as its figurehead, should firmly signal its progressiveness and modernity by adopting English, not Latin, as the language of its services. As a result, in 1549 a new *Book of Common Prayer* was published and sent to every church parish in England, ultimately transforming the words and prayers of every church service in the country overnight. The response among the English people to the change was one of shock and immense discontent.

The fallout from the introduction of this *Book of Common Prayer* was felt especially in the counties of Devon and Cornwall, in the far southwest corner of England. Not only were there religious and liturgical questions to be answered (the *Book of Common Prayer* demonstrated a noticeable shift towards Protestantism, which did not go down well in the predominantly Catholic counties of the southwest), but in Cornwall in particular there was a cultural problem too. The main language of Cornwall at the time was not English but Cornish—a Celtic language, closer in structure to Welsh, Scots, and Irish. Being forced to hold church services in English, ultimately, was seen as an uncomfortable and unwanted imposition on the people of Cornwall, and as a result, the county quickly rose in protest.

The unrest in Cornwall soon spread to the neighboring County of Devon and by July 1549 a combined force of Cornish and Devonian rebels, believed to number as many as 6,000 people, besieged and took control of the city of Exeter, the largest town and de facto capital of the region. For more than a month the protestors controlled the city, and held back repeated attempts by King Edward's troops to expel them and quash the rebellion. Eventually, however, after more than six weeks' unrest, Edward's forces successfully cut off food supplies to the city. Facing starvation, the protestors were compelled to surrender. With many of those who had sparked the uprising now killed or imprisoned, what became known as the Prayer Book Rebellion—and yet another curious chapter in the history of England—was finally over.

CHAPTER 4

A BRIDGE TOO TALL

The battle between the decimal metric system and the more old-fashioned (and mathematically taxing) imperial system of weights and measures is a longstanding one.

One of the many advantages of the metric system is its simplicity: units like meters and grams are counted in 10s, 100s, and 1000s, while the older imperial system—though more traditional, and with many centuries of use behind it— relies on less straightforward units like the 8 pints in a gallon, the 12 inches in a foot, and the 16 ounces in a pound.

But as arithmetically tricky as numbers like 8, 12 and 14 are to work with, they seem effortlessly easy compared to a bizarre unit of measurement called the *smoot*—which is equal to 67 inches, or precisely 5 feet 7 inches.

So where has such a seemingly random measurement come from? The story behind it involves three factors: namely, a fraternity prank; the future Chairman of the American National Standards Institute; and the Harvard Bridge, connecting Boston and Cambridge over the Charles River in Eastern Massachusetts.

It was in October 1958 that 18-year-old MIT student Oliver R. Smoot was volunteered by some of his Lambda Chi Alpha fraternity brothers to measure the length of the Harvard Bridge from one end to the other. To carry out the survey, the students decided to use Smoot himself as the measuring device, and so had him lie down on the ground where his height of 5 feet 7 inches was marked on the sidewalk with chalk. He then stood up, walked up to the chalk mark, and lay down on the sidewalk again, so his height could once more be marked onto the concrete. And so it went on, one measurement at a time, from one side of the bridge to the other. Eventually, after more than an hour of work, it was discovered that the Harvard Bridge was in total some 364.4 "smoots" in length (give or take a head or two).

The prank soon became the stuff of legend at MIT, and Smoot's contribution to investigative surveying has not gone unnoticed in and around campus. To this day, graffiti on the Harvard Bridge still divides the structure up into several hundred Smoot-based sections. A plaque commemorating the 50th anniversary of the stunt was unveiled on the bridge in 2008. And in 2011—several years after Oliver R. Smoot had been made chairman of the American National Standards Institute—the word *smoot* was added to the *American Heritage Dictionary*, defined as "a unit of measurement equal to five feet, seven inches."

All told, the smoot must surely be one of the most ludicrously precise units of measurement ever recorded in the English dictionary, even when compared to the imperial system!

CHAPTER 5

SHADY DEALINGS

In 2007, a team of scientists and engineers based at the English research company Surrey NanoSystems made an extraordinary breakthrough.

Using a new technique involving so-called "vertically aligned nanotubules" - tiny carbon-based structures that can be specifically arranged on their end - the Surrey scientists produced the darkest, blackest substance known to science.

They called their discovery "vantablack," basing its name on their "VANTA" nanotubule technology. Over the years that followed, they continued to improve and refine its production, adapting it into a usable, sprayable pigment, and honing their technology to such an extent that one billion of these carbon nanotubules, - tiny, microscopic strands of carbon, standing upright, essentially like blades of grass - could be crammed into one single square centimeter.

The reason that the pigment appears so black because photons (that is, individual particles of light) strike the surface of the vantablack and are unable to escape this sea of light-absorbing nanotubules, and so their energy is simply absorbed and converted into heat. Almost every wavelength of light, from infrared to ultraviolet and everything in between, is affected in the same way, meaning vantablack absorbs an incredible 99.965% of all visible light. Looking at it is like looking quite literally into a black hole as it appears blacker than any black you'll likely have ever seen.

Envisaging that their pigment could have countless real-world applications - from lining the optical chambers of deep-space telescopes to improving the performance of infrared cameras, the Surrey NanoSystems team announced their discovery to an eager scientific community in 2014. When happened next, however, could scarcely have been predicted.

With the darkest synthetic substance known to man now on the market, the laboratory soon began fielding calls from potential investors and clients all over the world who were all keen to utilize Surrey NanoSystems' discovery. And among the calls they received was one from contemporary British-Indian artist Anish Kapoor.

Kapoor has been exploring color, shape, and space in his extraordinary artworks since the early 1970s. He is the artist behind the giant reflective "bean" (properly called *Cloud Gate*) in the middle of Chicago's Millennium Park and the remarkable twisting, helter-skelter-like observation tower (known as *Orbit*) that became one of the centerpieces of the London 2012 Olympics. Awarded the Turner Prize in 1991 and knighted by the Queen in 2013, Kapoor is one of the art world's most famous and respected artists. So a phone call and a business proposition from him was something Surrey NanoSystems could scarcely ignore.

As a result, in 2014 Kapoor signed a contract with the Surrey team that granted him and his art studio the exclusive world rights to vantablack. The entire global supply of the darkest pigment known to science was now the exclusive property of one sole artist.

Needless to say, Kapoor's exclusive rights deal to the vantablack market did not go down too well with his fellow artists, and the move was quickly seen as uncharitably monopolizing and then shutting down an entirely new and exciting technology. On social media, campaigns were started to try to convince Kapoor to reverse his decision. Newspaper editorials around the world questioned just how acceptably 'right' was it for one artist alone to own something it would be impossible for any other artist to access or replicate. Others, meanwhile, questioned whether Kapoor's controversial actions were themselves a form of performance art.

But artists are a creative and reactionary bunch, of course, so it was not long before contemporary British artist Stuart Semple stepped into the fray with a take of his own on Kapoor's controversial move.

Stemple, who is known for his pop-art inspired works in a variety of different forms and media, reacted to the uproar surrounding Kapoor by creating an exclusive pigment of his own, which he named simply "PINK." According to a disclaimer on his website, Stemple claims that anyone can buy a supply of PINK so long as they are not Anish Kapoor.

"We all remember kids at school who wouldn't share their coloring pencils," Semple later explained. "Anish can have his black. But the rest of us will be playing with the rainbow!"

CHAPTER 6

YOU CAN COUNT ON IT

Cast your mind back to high school math lessons, and you'll no doubt be able to recall that prime numbers are numbers divisible only by themselves and 1 — like 13, 17, 19, and 23.

If you're not a mathematician, that's probably the only named set of digits that you can bring to mind, but prime numbers are just one of many quirkily-named groups of digits that math wizards have come up with. A so-called *abundant* number, for instance, is a number that is smaller than the sum of its divisors — so 12 is smaller than 1 + 2 + 3 + 4 + 6, which totals 16. If a number is equal to the total of its divisors, then it's called a *perfect* number — like 6, which equals 1 + 2 + 3. *Cousin* numbers are pairs of prime numbers that are four digits apart, like 3 and 7, or 7 and 11. *Twin primes* differ by just two (like 3 and 5, or 5 and 7), while pairs of prime numbers that are six places apart (like 5 and 11) are somewhat colorfully known as *sexy* primes. But of all the quirky number names in the mathematical textbooks, perhaps one of the strangest — and the most complex — is the *taxicab* number.

Taxicab numbers are numbers that can be expressed as the sum of two cubes in two different ways. In other words, a number, x, can be called a taxicab so long as $x = a^3 + b^3$ and $c^3 + d^3$. If you can replace the - a, b, c, and d in those equations with four different whole numbers there, then you've got a taxicab.

These kinds of numbers are extraordinarily rare, and incredibly only six taxicabs have ever been discovered. The first and smallest of these is technically 2 - because it is the sum of the reversible calculation $1^3 + 1^3$. After that, you won't come across another taxicab number until you reach 1,789 - which is equal to both $1^3 + 12^3$, and $9^3 + 10^3$. From there, the third taxicab number is 87,539,319; the fourth is 6,963,472,309,248; and the fifth is 48,988,659,276,962,496. The sixth and largest taxicab number yet discovered as yet - 24,153,319,581,254,312,065,344 - was identified as recently as 2003. (That's just over 24 sextillions, should you want to read it out!)

But one question remains: Why are these numbers called *taxicabs*?

This particular story begins with a British mathematician and Cambridge University scholar named GH Hardy, and his longtime friend and mathematical research collaborator, the Indian mathematician Srinivasa Ramanujan. Together, Hardy and Ramanujan first began working on numerous mathematical projects in 1913 by postal communication, when Ramanujan initially sent nine pages of mind-boggling handwritten mathematical formulae from his home in India to Hardy's office at Cambridge. Impressed by Ramanujan's obvious natural talent for numbers, Hardy arranged for him to travel to England to meet, and the pair soon began several years' worth of highly productive collaboration.

In the late 1910s, Ramanujan suddenly took ill and was hospitalized in London. On hearing the news, Hardy quickly took the train from Cambridge, and then jumped into a cab at the station to head straight to the hospital to see him. To pass the time on his cab journey across the city, Hardy began pondering what mathematical properties the number of the taxicab he happened to have caught — 1789 — might have.

On arriving at the hospital, Hardy told Ramanujan that he was a bit dismayed that the number 1789 seemed to him to be a "rather dull" number, with few interesting properties — and that he hoped its apparent dreariness wasn't an "unfavorable omen" for his friend's medical treatment. "No," Ramanujan replied, with a smile. "It is actually a very interesting number: it is the smallest number expressible as the sum of two cubes in two different ways."

Numbers sharing this peculiar quality have since become known as "taxicabs" — while the number 1789 itself is now known as the "Hardy-Ramanujan" number in honor of its unlikely discoverers. Today, it is just one of several mathematical first that bear this extraordinary duo's names.

CHAPTER 7

DISASTER AREA

Historians tend to disagree about the precise start date of the so-called Colonial Era—when many of the major seafaring nations of Western Europe began to travel around the world establishing new trade routes and eventually imposing (often violently and uncompromisingly) their control over the rest of the globe. No matter when this era is said to have begun, by the late 1500s and early 1600s, a handful of European countries - most notably England, France, Spain, and Portugal were already exercising their power over vast swathes of the globe, from Central and South America to parts of Africa, India, the Pacific Ocean, and the Far East.

There is at least one more European country that can be said to have become involved in this era of exploration and expansion, but whose contribution to colonialism is long-forgotten, often overlooked, and not particularly well known. Namely, the Kingdom of Scotland.

Several years before, under the Act of Union, which brought Scotland and England together to form the beginnings of the UK in 1707, Scotland was effectively an independent, self-governing nation. Additionally, seeing how successfully its

English neighbor to the south was expanding its rule around the world, Scotland understandably also wanted a piece of the colonial pie.

In the early 1690s, moves began to be made to establish a Scottish-run colony somewhere in the Americas that would be known as "New Caledonia" (literally "New Scotland"). There, from a newly-established colonial capital called "New Edinburgh," Scottish-made produce could be traded and exchanged locally with both the native Americans and fellow colonialists, thereby bolstering the Scottish economy back home and boosting the country's status worldwide.

A site near Darien, in modern-day Panama, was selected as the prime location for New Caledonia, and a hugely successful Scots entrepreneur named Sir William Paterson was placed in charge of the project. As well as being one of the co-founders of the Bank of England, Paterson was also a successful tradesman in his own right, having already established several privately-operated trade routes across the Atlantic Ocean linking ports in Scotland to trade posts across North America and the West Indies. A new trading corporation known as the Company of Scotland was founded in 1693, in order to organize New Caledonia, and with its backing, Paterson began to secure funding and investment from similar companies in England and continental Europe. Before long, thousands of pounds of investment had been raised—but just as the so-called Darien Scheme was about to be launched, Paterson's funding collapsed.

Fearing competition for their own overseas trading ventures and monopolies (most notably the infamous East India

Company), Paterson's English and Dutch backers suddenly got cold feet and began to pull out just weeks before his ships were due to set sail across the Atlantic. In characteristically undeterred fashion, however, Paterson simply turned closer to home for more investment and began petitioning the Scots people themselves to finance his wildly ambitious scheme.

Incredibly, the people of Scotland did precisely that in extraordinary numbers. Thousands of ordinary Scottish citizens went on to invest more than half a million pounds of capital in Paterson's colonial enterprise, while many hundreds more volunteered to man the fleet of ships that he and his crew would take to the Americas to establish New Caledonia. By the time the fleet set sail from Leith harbor, in Edinburgh, on July 12, 1698, Paterson had assembled more than 1,200 volunteers, and invested almost half the available national capital of the entire country in his project.

Clearly, the so-called Darien Scheme was to prove a make-or-break investment. And unfortunately for Scotland, it soon proved to be more of a "break" than a "make."

By the time the Scottish fleet arrived in Panama several weeks later, many of the Darien Scheme's crew were desperately ill, while some (including Paterson's wife) had even perished on the uncomfortable trans-Atlantic crossing. So, far from their arrival in the New World being a triumphant one marked by the breaking of new ground, the Scots colonists' first task was to dig a huge graveyard for the scores of crew members who had died enroute.

The situation was worsened further, as it soon transpired that few people involved in the Darien Scheme even knew the area in which they had landed, and its choice as the location of Scotland's new colony was, it seemed, based on little more than conjecture and anecdotal evidence rather than geographical and cartographical surveys. The area was intolerably difficult to live in, with mosquito-infested swamps and vast swathes of infertile, uncultivable land, wholly unsuited to both farming or building. What is more, Spanish settlers in the area did not take kindly to a rival set of colonists, and repeatedly and violently attacked the Scottish arrivals; ironically, far from finding themselves at war with the local tribespeople, it was the native Americans who helped the Darien settlers the most, bringing them gifts of fruit, bedding, and traditional medicines.

Despite this welcome assistance from the locals, however, the Darien Scheme proved disastrous. As time went by, scores more crew members fell ill with fever, leaving too few people healthy enough to establish any kind of base. Desperately ill and stuck in an inhospitable and impracticable location, eventually the decision was made to abandon New Caledonia and return home. Scotland's sole colonial venture was over.

CHAPTER 8

CRAZY FACTS 1

1. More people learn the Irish language online around the world than there are Irish speakers in Ireland.

2. According to a 2018 study by Google, people in Maine use Google to check the spelling of Connecticut more than any other word.

3. A group of pandas is called an embarrassment.

4. The planet Mercury is shrinking.

5. In 1987, an FBI agent named Robert Hanssen was tasked with rooting out a KGB mole from inside the organization; but in fact, he was the mole and had been working for Russia since 1979.

6. Hammerhead sharks were originally called "balance fish."

7. As a child, Justin Bieber learned to play the trumpet.

8. October 20 is International Sloth Day.

9. The @ sign was officially added to the Morse code alphabet in 2004 to make it possible to transmit email addresses via telegraphy.

10. Frank Sinatra had a scar on his face and a cauliflower ear caused by the forceps used on his mother when he was born.

11. The Romans were so good at using aqueducts to direct water that they sometimes used them to flood their arenas and stage indoor sea battles.

12. The Pyramids are both the oldest of the Seven Wonders of the World, and the only one still standing.

13. Sheryl Crow wrote her Bond theme *Tomorrow Never Dies* in 15 minutes.

14. On average, plastic shopping bags take 1,000 years to biodegrade.

15. Willie Nelson wrote the lyrics to his song *On the Road Again* on the back of an airplane sickness bag.

CHAPTER 9

LIFTING THE VEIL

The wedding of Prince Charles and Lady Diana Spencer in 1981 was one of the most memorable in modern royal history. While more than 750 million viewers around the world watched the ceremony on their television sets, a further 600,000 people lined the procession route through the streets of London, hoping to catch a glimpse of the royal couple as they made their way through the city, heading to St Paul's Cathedral. There, a congregation of 2,700 people — including dignitaries and heads of state from all around the world — watched the heir to the British throne marry a young woman destined, at that time, to be Britain's next queen.

One of the most memorable aspects of Charles and Diana's big day was Diana's wedding dress. Designed in absolute secrecy by legendary English fashion designers David and Elizabeth Emanuel, Diana wore an ivory-colored gown of silk-taffeta, hand-woven antique lace and crinoline, embellished with 10,000 individually sewn pearls and dramatic puffed sleeves, and followed by a 25-foot train that could barely fit inside the royal carriage. (Royal bridesmaid India Hicks, a member of the legendary Mountbatten dynasty, later recalled "trying as best as I could to de-wrinkle the situation" as Diana stepped down from the carriage to enter the cathedral.) The elaborate design, which went on to be credited with establishing a trend for over-the-top wedding gowns in the 1980s, also featured what is claimed to be the longest veil in the history of royal weddings: extending far beyond the dress' already immense train, the veil comprised a single 153-yard length of fine quality tulle. Diana's bridesmaids, again, had a mammoth task ensuring it looked perfect and had rehearsed for the big day by practicing folding an enormous cotton sheet.

Lady Diana's veil might have been longer than the length of a football pitch, but incredibly it is not the largest veil in the record books. According to the *Guinness Book of Records*, that particular title belongs to Cypriot bride Maria Paraskeva, whose veil on her wedding day in August 2018 was almost 50 times longer than that of Lady Diana's. In fact, in total, it was more than four miles in length.

Determined to ensure that her wedding day ended up a record-breaking event, Paraskeva spent a year sourcing factories, fabric-makers, tailors, and local seamstresses who could make her fairytale idea a reality. Eventually, she found a company in Greece who was willing to manufacture eight immense 1,000m rolls of high-quality tulle fabric — over three months — which Paraskeva then had sewn together by a team of local tailors in Cyprus to create one single seemingly never-ending veil. The entire manufacturing process alone cost her around 4,000 euros (equivalent to $4,600).

Once the manufacturers and seamstresses' work was

complete, the veil was taken via pickup truck to a local school field in the town of Larnaca, Cyprus, where it was slowly unrolled and pinned down to the ground by a team of 30 volunteers so that its entire length could be measured. A local civil engineer and quantity surveyor were called on to ensure that the measurements were accurate, and together they reckoned the entire veil measured an incredible 22,843 feet, 2.11 inches—equivalent to more than 60 football fields, or 76 times the height of the Statue of Liberty! Paraskeva's place in the record books was very easily assured.

CHAPTER 10

GOING DOWN A STORM

William Shakespeare famously based a number of his history plays on real-life characters from the past, including the English Kings Richard III, Henry V, and Henry VI; legendary figures like King Lear and Cymbeline, an ancient king of Britain; and Roman generals and leaders, like Titus Andronicus, Coriolanus, and Julius Caesar. But of all his remaining plays -namely, the comedies and tragedies - at least one is believed to have at least some grounding in an actual historical event.

According to legend, Shakespeare's *The Tempest*; generally taken to be the last play on which he worked prior to his death, was based on a contemporary true-life story of a shipwreck that had gripped England in the early 1600s. How much of the actual story Shakespeare chose to use in his play is, however, open to debate, especially given that his play takes place on an enchanted island overseen by a powerful sorcerer and his circle of supernatural assistants!

In the play, Prospero, the rightful heir to the dukedom of Milan, has been stranded on the unnamed island for more than a decade, having been double-crossed and set adrift at sea with his daughter Miranda by his brother Antonio, who has usurped his throne back in Milan. Having washed up on the shore of the island, Prospero uses his knowledge of magic and the supernatural to summon a band of spirits; including the fleet-footed Ariel and the monstrous Caliban, to help him and his daughter survive. When a storm wrecks another ship from Milan on the island's reefs, Prospero uses his magic to both keep the vessel safe in its harbor and divide its motley crew into groups, all as part of a grand plan to reclaim his throne and take back control of Milan.

Prospero's magical powers and his merry band of sprites and spirits aren't, of course, rooted in any real-life sorcery. But the shipwreck that crashes upon his island almost certainly was.

On June 2, 1609, a ship named the *Sea Venture* set sail from Portsmouth, on the south coast of England, as part of a vast fleet of ships heading for Jamestown in Virginia. After nearly two months at sea, on July 24 the fleet sailed directly into an enormous tropical storm, and while the majority of its ships headed northwards to escape the hurricane, the *Sea Venture* became separated from the group. Lost at sea, she and her crew were left to face the full force of the storm alone.

The ship's captain, Sir George Somers, was left with only one option. He intentionally steered the ship towards the only solid land that he and his 150 passengers and fellow crew members had seen for weeks and deliberately ran the *Sea Venture* aground on what is now Bermuda. For the next nine months, the survivors of the *Sea Venture* were left stranded on the island, with no means of letting the outside world know that, thanks to Captain Somers' actions, they had indeed survived the storm.

During those nine months, Somers and his surviving crewmen used the wreckage of the *Sea Venture* (along with some timber sourced from the island itself) to construct two smaller vessels, which they named the *Deliverance* and *Patience*. Eventually, they were deemed seaworthy, and the survivors of the *Sea Venture* set sail once more; and finally reached Jamestown on May 23, 1610 — almost a year after they had first left England.

On their arrival in America, news of the incredible ordeal and survival of the *Sea Venture* and her passengers caused a sensation, and as a result, soon reached England. In 1610, an English writer named William Strachey, who had been one of the passengers on the *Sea Venture*, published what he called his *True Reportory*, a 24,000-word account of the "wracke and redemption" of the ship, and its eventual miraculous arrival in Jamestown. Believing that Shakespeare likely began work on the script for *The Tempest* sometime in late 1610–early 1611, many Shakespearean scholars now believe that it's likely Strachey's account (or, at least, an account very similar to it) may indeed have provided him with the inspiration he needed for the last of his astonishing plays.

Whether it did or did not, however, remains debatable — but there is, at least, one more thing that is most definitely inspired by the *Sea Venture*'s remarkable tale of survival: to this day, the flag of Bermuda depicts a ship being wrecked upon the island's shores.

CHAPTER 11

HAT TRICK

What do Abraham Lincoln, Mr. Peanut, and Rich Uncle Pennybags from the *Monopoly* game all have in common?

The answer, of course, is their headgear. All three are well known for wearing a top hat; or in President Lincoln's case, the even more impressive stovepipe.

According to fashion legend, the top hat was invented by an English haberdasher named John Hetherington in the winter of 1797. Supposedly, Hetherington owned a hat-making stall on the Strand in the City of Westminster, in central London, and it was there that he designed a new and striking style of elongated headwear, cylindrical in shape with a broad, stiff brim, and made of rich and lustrous black silk.

Whether or not that history is entirely accurate is somewhat open to question, but it nevertheless appears to be the case that Hetherington was indeed the first person to *wear* a top hat while walking around the streets of London. And we know that because Hetherington's choice of headgear eventually landed him in trouble with the law.

Allegedly, it was on the morning of January 16, 1797, that

Hetherington decided to premiere his new creation by stepping out of his shop and walking around the streets of London wearing his top hat, to drum up some new business. It's certainly true that his design turned more than a few heads; but as he continued to walk, the stir he created behind him eventually transformed into a full-scale riot.

"Several women fainted at the unusual sight," recorded one contemporary report, reproduced by the *Hatter's Gazette* almost a century later. "Children screamed, dogs barked," and the young son of a local cordwainer (i.e. shoemaker) was "thrown down by the crowd which had collected [around Hetherington] and had his right arm broken" in the melee. Eventually, the ruckus caused by Hetherington's hat caught the attention of a group of police constables, who had him arrested and taken to the Lord Mayor—along with his top hat—on a charge of breaching the peace.

In his defense, Hetherington claimed that he was not breaking any laws but was "merely exercising a right to appear in a head-dress of his own design," something which he decreed was "a right not denied to any Englishman." The Lord Mayor, it seems, did not share Hetherington's relaxed attitude, and when his hat was displayed to the court as evidence, its design was deemed to be "calculated to frighten timid people."

Hetherington was found guilty of appearing "on the public highway wearing upon his head what he called a silk hat … a tall structure having a shiny luster," and as recompense ordered to pay bonds totaling £500—a staggering amount for the time, equivalent to more than £60,000 ($82,000) today.

Hetherington's hat might have landed him in trouble back in

1797, but the design nevertheless caught on. Before long, elongated top hats began to grow in popularity (and we can presume, become somewhat less scandalous and frightening), and by the 19th century were considered the height of fashion in upper-class society. Hetherington's place in their history, meanwhile, eventually became the stuff of legend.

CHAPTER 12

PARLEZ–VOUS FRANÇAIS

Chances are that, at some point in your life, you'll have enjoyed a game of *Scrabble*—the tricky word-connecting board game developed in the 1930s, in which players build words from differently-valued lettered tiles in an attempt to outscore and outplay one another. If you're something of a word nerd, you might even be fairly proficient at playing it, and making the most of all of its high-scoring Q's, Z's, and J's, and playing your words across triple-word and double-letter squares to score as big a total as possible. Of course, if you're not much of a word nerd, you might instead find yourself staring hopelessly at a rack of 7 E's, or struggling to play anything of more than three letters, or score more than double figures...

To its fans and players around the world, *Scrabble* is a big deal. Games are sold in more than two dozen different languages and in over 120 different countries around the world. *Scrabble* clubs and competitions attract tens of thousands of players each year, and an annual Scrabble Champions Tournament (formerly the bi-annual World Scrabble Championship) attracts the very best players from the very best contests from all around the globe. With *Scrabble* such a global phenomenon, of course, different contests are held for speakers of different languages—each of which has different rules, sets of lettered tiles, and lists of permissible words. In 2015, however, the lines between these different competitions were blurred by a truly remarkable player.

New Zealand native Nigel Richards already had a handful of English-language *Scrabble* titles to his name when he entered himself into the French-language Scrabble World Championships in Louvain-la-Neuve, in Belgium, in July 2015. As a truly talented player, Richards quickly swept his way to the final, and despite some truly unlucky and challenging racks of letters, was eventually crowned World Champion—becoming the first person in competitive Scrabble history to hold a world title in two different languages.

What makes Richards' 2015 victory all the more remarkable, however, is that he doesn't actually speak French. "He just learned the words," one of Richards' friends confessed to the *New Zealand Herald* at the time. "He won't know what they mean [and] wouldn't be able to carry out a conversation in French."

So how do you win a French *Scrabble* competition—against some of the best French-speaking *Scrabble* players in the world—if you don't actually speak the language?

The answer, it seems, is simply to memorize as many of the 386,000 words that are permissible in French *Scrabble* play as possible. The words' meanings, their grammar, and their uses in French writing and conversation are all unnecessary complications, none of which needs to be known. All that matters, simply, is the string of letters from which they are comprised.

Nine weeks before the competition date, Richards did precisely that and set about memorizing as much French vocabulary as possible. In that way, the game became more a challenge of mathematical strategy and gameplay than vocabulary or language. As French journalist and *Scrabble* fan Jean-Baptiste Morel wrote of Richards' victory at the time, he "learned no language logic" in preparing for his victory, but rather, "just a succession of letter sequences giving rise to words. In his head it's binary: what draw of letters can make a *Scrabble*, and what draw can't."

So next time you're struggling to get rid of a Q, K, Z, and V all in one go—or find yourself stuck playing words like *dog* and *man*—you can at least be grateful that you're playing in your own native tongue.

CHAPTER 13

A DOG IN THE HUNT

To soccer fans around the world, the Jules Rimet Trophy is one of the most famous and important trophies in all of sport. Named after the third president of soccer's ruling body FIFA, the Jules Rimet Trophy was for many years the top prize in the FIFA World Cup competition, awarded to the contest's winner every four years, beginning with the very first champions, Uruguay, in 1930.

In the decades that followed, the trophy was handed out to whichever national soccer team won this most prestigious of association football competitions. And as befits such a high-status competition, the trophy itself is a remarkably impressive prize.

Standing more than 14 inches tall, the Jules Rimet is made from 18-carat gold-plated sterling silver, decorated around its base with rich green lapis lazuli stone, and depicts the Greek goddess of victory, Nike, holding a globe in her outstretched arms. That design remained in place right up until the 1970s when Brazil won the FIFA World Cup for a record third time. As per the competition's rules at the time—and as stipulated by Jules Rimet himself, back in the 1930s—that victory ultimately allowed the Brazilian team to hold on to the trophy in perpetuity, and as a result, a new trophy (of almost identical) design was commissioned. Teams today compete for what is officially known simply as the FIFA World Cup Trophy, which has been awarded at every competition from 1974 to the present day.

That long and impressive history of one of sport's most equally impressive trophies was, however, interrupted for several weeks in the mid-1960s. The 1966 FIFA World Cup winners were England, who took the title for both the first time in their own history and the World Cup competition's history. Played on home turf at Wembley Stadium in London—and in front of an audience of 96,000 spectators, with more than 30 million people watching at home—the English team swept to a decisive 4–2 victory against long-time rivals West Germany on July 30. After the game, England captain Bobby Moore (who was later knighted for his contribution to England's victory) made his way up into the Wembley stands and was handed the Jules Rimet Trophy by Queen Elizabeth II.

A few months earlier, however, the chances of that presentation ever being able to take place were thrown into considerable doubt.

In January 1966, several months before that year's World Cup competition got under-way, the Jules Rimet Trophy arrived in London and was handed over to England's Football Association organization for safekeeping. The following month, the FA agreed to loan the trophy out to an exhibition to be held at Westminster Central Hall in London and thereby allow fans from across the country to come and catch a glimpse of one of soccer's most illustrious prizes. The exhibition, with the Jules Rimet Trophy as its main attraction, opened on March 19, 1966; but the following day, the case in which it was kept was jimmied open and the trophy stolen.

Scotland Yard was quickly put in charge of the case, and news broke of the theft the following morning. Descriptions of two suspects—suspicious characters sighted in the vicinity of the exposition the previous day—were handed to the press, but little progress had been made on the case before a parcel containing the removable gilt lining from the top of the trophy arrived on the doorstep of Joe Mears, the Chairman of England's Football Association. Alongside the parcel was a note demanding a ransom of £15,000 cash—equivalent to more than a quarter of a million pounds ($350,000) today—in exchange for the safe return of the trophy. The perpetrators explained that the cash should be left in a specific location, inside a leather briefcase, by the following Friday, or else they would melt the trophy down and it would never be seen again.

With the help of the police, Mears went along with the thieves' demands, and a decoy briefcase containing a few genuine banknotes padded out with reams of worthless scrap paper was used in a swiftly-arranged sting operation just a few days later. On March 24, a petty thief and used car dealer named Edward Betchley, was arrested and charged with both the theft of the trophy, and a separate charge of breaking and entering. Betchley, however, claimed to be little more than a paid middleman in the exchange, and explained that he had been given a fee of £500 to act on behalf of a third party - the true thief - who had been known only to him as "The Pole."

Only he, Betchley claimed, knew the whereabouts of the trophy, and now that Betchley had been arrested there was no way of contacting this shady third party; or of recovering the Jules Rimet trophy.

In the trial that eventually followed, Betchley was found guilty of demanding money with intent to steal and received a two-year jail sentence. Scotland Yard's sting operation might have successfully caught at least one party in the theft of the World Cup trophy, but in apprehending Betchley, it seemed the police had also simultaneously lost the trophy for good.

Then, on March 27, something quite unexpected happened. A Londoner named David Corbett was walking his black and white collie dog - Pickles, in the Beulah Hill district of southeast London, when Pickles started to nose at a disheveled-looking parcel—wrapped in an old newspaper, and tied up with string—lying under the hedge of Corbett's house. Luckily, Corbett didn't merely dismiss the parcel as little more than litter and opened it up. Inside was the Jules Rimet Trophy.

The Trophy was handed in to a police station in nearby Gipsy Hill, London, and was held by the Metropolitan Police as evidence until the middle of April, when it was finally handed back to the Football Association for the run-up to the competition. As for Corbett—and, more importantly, Pickles the dog—they became heroes.

Corbett was awarded a £5,000 reward for finding the trophy, while Pickles was awarded the silver medal of the National Canine Defense League, gifted a year's worth of free dog food, and named "Dog of the Year" by pet food manufacturer Spillers. Pickles even went on to make a series of television

41

and film appearances, including the 1966 comedy crime caper, *The Spy with a Cold Nose*.

Sadly, Pickles died the following year. But for his extraordinary and unexpected contribution to world soccer, he is now memorialized in the park where the trophy was found with a special commemorative plaque, while his collar remains on display to this day in England's National Football Museum, in Manchester.

CHAPTER 14

BATTLE DRESS

From our *Achilles* tendon to our *zeppelin* airships, there are countless words in the dictionary that are named after characters, both real and invented, from throughout history and literature. But if legend is to be believed, easily one of the most unusual stories in the dictionary is that which lies behind both the name of a color called *isabelline*, and the European princess, Infanta Isabella, who inspired it.

Isabelline is the name of a pale, ruddy, yellowish-brown color. It's unlikely to be a word you'll have ever come across unless you're an animal lover: it tends only to be used in the names of creatures like the Isabelline wheatear, an Asian songbird, and the Isabelline bear, a pale-colored subspecies of brown bear found in the Himalayas. As for its namesake, she too will be fairly unknown to most people: the Isabella in question is Isabella Clara Eugenia, the young daughter of King Phillip II of Spain and his third wife, Elisabeth of Valois, and an early 17th-century Habsburg ruler of the Spanish Netherlands.

Unless you're an expert on the Habsburg monarchs of Europe, it's unlikely that any of the names in that description will ring many bells—although Isabella's father, Philip II, was for a time in the mid-1500s married to Mary I of England, the elder sister of Elizabeth I, making him a *de facto* king of Tudor England. This particular tale, however, takes place some three years after Philip's own death, in 1601.

The dying King Philip II had made provisions in his will to bequeath rule of the Spanish Netherlands—a vast province of the northern Holy Roman Empire, comprising parts of modern-day France, Belgium, Luxembourg, Holland, and Germany—to Isabella, on the condition that she marry and thereby jointly rule with her cousin Albert VII, the Archduke of Austria. The pair duly married in 1599, and assumed joint control of the Spanish Netherlands at a particularly turbulent point in its history.

By the late 1500s, the Spanish Netherlands and its surrounding states had been embroiled in a bitter conflict that would eventually become known as the Eighty Years' War, and go on to subsume much of western Europe. The Dutch, unhappy with Spain's rule over the area (and the proliferation of Spanish Catholicism that went with it), had started to rebel against the Spanish control, and after an allied Dutch force retook the city of Groningen from the Spanish throne in 1568, war promptly broke out.

In response, Spain was quick to react and spent the next decade reasserting Spanish rule over much of the southern provinces of the Spanish Netherlands in a series of bloody battles and sieges. To survive the war without being subsumed entirely into the Spanish crown, the Dutch clearly needed allies and assistance—and in 1585 they got it.

Fearing the threat to English soil that a Spanish victory just across the English Channel would pose, Elizabeth I agreed to lend England's support to the Dutch rebels. The Spanish, now essentially battling two powerful military forces at once, had a fight on their hands. As the conflict rumbled on, the Spanish forces became increasingly desperate to find some way of demonstrating and reasserting their power over the area; and eventually, all eyes fell on the only Dutch-controlled city remaining in the entire region: the Flemish city of Ostend.

The Spanish knew that retaking Ostend would prove an immense boost of morale to the flagging Spanish forces, and could help to tip the wartime balance against the English and Dutch. As a result, on July 5, 1601, Isabella's husband, Albert of Austria, besieged the city with an army of 12,000 troops, easily outnumbering the 3,000 or so people (mainly impoverished fishermen and their families) who lived inside. Victory, it seemed, would come quickly.

Back home in Spain, Isabella was waiting patiently for news of her husband's efforts in the war further north, and when news arrived that he was finally in a position to besiege and claim back control of Ostend, Isabella became convinced the conflict would soon be over. Indeed, she apparently became so sure of her husband's imminent victory that she made an agreement with one of her handmaids (or, in other versions of the story, one of her husband's counselors) to not change her undergarments until after Ostend had fallen under Spanish control. It seemed like an easy victory, both for Albert and for Isabella: surely a destitute fishing town of only a few thousand people could scarcely hold back the Spanish army? Within a few days, Isabella wagered, news would surely arrive of her husband's victory.

In fact, she could scarcely have been more wrong.

Back in Ostend, Albert was facing a series of difficulties. Firstly, as the only Dutch controlled enclave still standing in the region, the Dutch forces had seen fit to bolster both Ostend's defenses (which by upgrading its surrounding walls had been transformed into a series of battlements more befitting a military camp than a sleepy coastal resort) and its population (by ferrying more than 4,500 Dutch troops into the town). Not only that, but as a major fishing port, the north end of Ostend was open to the North Sea, and that vital channel enabled much needed military supplies, chiefly from across the Channel in England, to be ferried almost continually into the town.

Surrounding this maritime gateway, moreover, was a vast expanse of nearly impenetrable mudflats and quicksand, making this vital supply chain all but impossible to break from on land. Archduke Albert, ultimately, was with little option but to concentrate all of his Spanish forces onto the much more heavily-defended southern side of the town. Victory, if it were ever to come, was not going to come easy. The Siege of Ostend went on to last for some 1,173 days.

The Spanish finally proved victorious and retook the town in September 1604, but at an immense cost to their campaign. Thousands of Spanish troops had been killed. The Spanish treasury had been all but emptied. While having concentrated so fixedly on securing victory only in Ostend, in the meantime, the equally important Spanish-held port of Sluis, 20 miles to the east, had fallen to the Dutch and English forces. In the end, securing control of Ostend proved a hollow victory, and with few options remaining open to them, the Spanish called a halt to the war. An uneasy 12-year truce commenced.

In all this time, of course, Isabella reportedly remained true to her word and refused to change her underclothes until her husband had proved victorious. After more than one thousand days of brutal fighting and attrition, ultimately, her crisp, white undergarments were not quite as spotless as they had once been.

As a result—in perhaps one of the strangest word origin tales in the dictionary—Infanta Isabella ended up giving her name not to a pristine shade of white, but to a sandy, beige-like shade of yellow…

CHAPTER 15

KING OF THE BEASTS

A vast castle and ancient fortress located on the north bank of the Thames—just along from its equally impressive namesake, Tower Bridge—the Tower of London is one of England's most famous and most recognizable landmarks, as well as one of the capital's most popular tourist attractions.

Built in the 11th century, today the Tower of London is an official royal palace under direct ownership of the British Crown and is well known as the storehouse and exhibition space of the royal family's Crown Jewels. The Jewels have been on display in their current location, in the Tower's specialist Jewel House, since 1994—but incredibly, the tradition of keeping them at the Tower dates back as far as the 13th century.

Over its almost 1,000 year history, however, the Tower has been used as a lot more than a safe house for the royal jewel collection. In fact, the Tower has operated under several different guises down the centuries—including as a prison, an armory, a public records office, a treasury, and even a royal mint, where new coins and cash could be produced under the watchful eye of the monarch and their court. But of all the

Tower's myriad uses over the years, perhaps its most surprising is that it was once home to a vast medieval menagerie. And perhaps one of the Tower's most surprising inhabitants in that time was a gigantic polar bear.

The first monarch known to have kept animals in the menagerie at the Tower of London is believed to be the medieval King John, who ruled England from 1199 until his death in 1216, one year after the signing of the Magna Carta. It was during John's reign that a series of payroll records cataloged at the Tower makes reference to a staff of "lion keepers" who were employed at the Tower in the years 1210–1212. Precisely what happened to King John's lions is unclear; as is precisely how prepared his 13th-century courtiers were to look after some gigantic man-eating cats! But when John's successor, Henry III, was presented with a further three leopards as a wedding gift from the Holy Roman Emperor, Frederick II, in 1235, he decided that all these extraordinary creatures should henceforth form the centerpieces of a new exotic Royal Menagerie, housed entirely at the Tower of London.

In the later part of his reign in the mid-1200s, Henry oversaw the construction of a considerable extension to the Tower of London purely intended to house wild animals, and throughout his time on the throne, the number of animals kept at the Tower grew considerably. His leopards and King John's lions were eventually joined by a pair of European lynxes, monkeys, a pack of wild dogs and hounds, and even an elephant—perhaps the first elephant not only seen in England but in all of northern Europe—that was a gift from the King of France, Louis IX, in 1255. But of all the creatures in the royal collection, King Henry's polar bear was by far the most impressive.

The bear was added to the collection in 1251, when the Norwegian king, Haakon IV, gifted it to Henry to cement a friendly alliance between the two great kingdoms. The polar bear understandably caused quite a stir in London at the time — not least because King Henry decided that it should not remain locked in its cage in the Tower all day, but should be allowed down to the banks of the river Thames each day to swim, bathe, exercise, and catch fish.

As a result, in 1252 the King issued an order for an iron muzzle and chain leash, which the bear's fearless keepers were then left to somehow fit to the creature and thereby lead through the streets beside the Tower and down to the riverside every morning. Once the bear had had its fill of fish and had duly enjoyed enough time frolicking in the water, it would then be hauled back out of the river, back up to the Tower, and returned to its enclosure for the remainder of the day.

Unfortunately, we do not know for how many years this daily bear show took place, as the fates of many of the animals that inhabited the Tower of London in the early days of its menagerie are unknown. We do know, however, that a royal menagerie of some description was maintained at the Tower of London for the next six centuries, right up to the reign of Queen Victoria in the mid-1800s. In that time, the Kings' bear, leopards, and lions were further joined by a cheetah, hyenas, tigers, kangaroos, jackals, eagles, ostriches, camels, wolves, zebras, pumas, an alligator, and even a troop of baboons — one of whom, according to a contemporary description, even learned how to smoke a clay pipe.

Not all of the Tower's animals, however, appear to have been kept under as strict control as Henry's polar bear. In 1686 a lady named Mary Jenkinson who worked in the keepers' house at the menagerie, took one of her acquaintances in to see the Tower's lions. When one of the lions reportedly stretched out a paw towards her, Mary unwisely went to stroke it. According to a report, the lion then "catched her by the middle of the arm with his claws and mouth," and wrenched her arm clean off her body. Despite a desperate struggle to save her, Mary was killed.

Other incidents recorded over the years include a wolf that escaped and killed the pet dog of a Sergeant Cropper who worked at the tower; a baboon that somehow came into possession of a cannonball and threw it at a soldier, killing him; a boa constrictor that escaped its enclosure and throttled a zookeeper; and a young boy in 1810, who had his leg torn off by another baboon; incredibly, there were no enclosures at all in the Tower's monkey house, meaning members of the public could walk right up to the animals (and, it seems, vice versa).

By that time, interest in the menagerie was dwindling, and concerns over both the welfare of the animals and the expense of keeping so many of them at the Tower led to the establishment of what is now London Zoo in 1826. The final 150 animals kept at the Tower went on to become the zoo's very first exhibits, while their housings and enclosures at the Tower were eventually demolished and their equipment auctioned off. Today, nothing remains of the Tower's menagerie except for a few life-size sculptures of some of its most famous animal residents.

CHAPTER 16

CRAZY FACTS 2

1. The Leaning Tower of Pisa started to lean while it was still being built.

2. In 2019, 46 million Australian banknotes were printed with the word "responsibility" misspelled "responsibilty."

3. Giraffes have the same number of bones in their necks as humans.

4. 1/100th of a second is called a jiffy.

5. The pilot episode of the television series *Lost* was so expensive that the executive who gave it the green light, was fired.

6. Cleopatra lived closer in time to the modern day than she did to the building of the Great Pyramid of Giza.

7. Legally, the Queen owns the United Kingdom's undersea continental shelf.

8. The first email sent by a US President was sent by Bill Clinton to an astronaut in space. President Clinton only sent one more email during his entire presidency.

9. Brad Pitt's ninth cousin is Barack Obama.

10. The novelist Marcel Proust's last words were "Thank you for getting the beer."

11. Every year, Thailand holds a gigantic buffet for wild monkeys.

12. The original Argentine tango was traditionally danced by two men.

13. The name Lego comes from a Danish word meaning "play well."

14. When the dinosaurs were walking the Earth, Saturn didn't have any rings.

15. The Ancient Egyptians used a preparation containing crocodile droppings as a form of birth control.

CHAPTER 17

A LOAD OF BUNKUM

"What a load of bunk!"

Nowadays, the word *bunk* has become such a familiar word for garbage or nonsensical language that we've even invented an opposite term – *debunk* - meaning to fact-check, or prove that something is untrue. As familiar as both those words are, however, few people know their history and the connection that *bunk* has to a particularly memorable Carolinian congressman.

Felix Walker was born in Hampshire, Virginia (now in West Virginia) in 1753. His family moved frequently throughout Virginia, the Carolinas, and the surrounding states in his childhood, and as a young man, Walker worked several different places throughout the region in various clerical and local government positions. In 1769, he was hired as a merchant's clerk in Charleston, South Carolina. He then joined Daniel Boone's company, helping to establish Boonesborough, Kentucky, in 1775, and was later named Clerk of the Court of Washington district, North Carolina, in 1775. After serving in the Revolutionary War, Walker returned to North Carolina and served in its state assembly numerous times before being

54

elected to the 15th United States Congress as the Democratic-Republican representative for Buncombe County, North Carolina, in 1816.

Walker went on to spend a total of six years in the House of Representatives, before stepping down in 1823, five years before his death in 1828 at the age of 75. It was during his time in Congress, however, that Walker — and, by extension, Buncombe County — made their somewhat unexpected contribution to our language.

In late 1819, Congress was tasked with debating the so-called Missouri Question: namely, whether the territory of Missouri should be admitted into the Union as a free or a slave state. The debate had already rumbled on for several inconclusive months until finally, just before a decisive vote was due to be taken early the following year, Congressman Walker stood to address the house on February 25, 1820. Far from bringing the debate to a convincing, vote-swinging conclusion, however, Walker went on to deliver an impossibly lengthy and almost entirely irrelevant 5,000-word speech.

"Mr. Speaker," he began, "I should not have risen on this question did I not believe that we are about to be plunged into a dangerous and conflicting policy wherein some of our best interests and dearest rights are deeply involved. In giving my views on this subject, I find I have to encounter difficulties that I cannot avoid." And so Congressman Walker went on, and on, and on, with his exasperated and exhausted colleagues, keen to conclude the debate and simply move on to the vote, repeatedly shouting him down and calling for him to cease talking. Despite their protests, however, Walker continued with his speech, proudly explaining that he was not delivering his address for their benefit, but was rather making a "speech for Buncombe."

So memorably useless and entirely unnecessary was Congressman Walker's speech, however, that "speaking for Buncombe" soon established itself as a slangy catchphrase around the House of Representatives—while the name *Buncombe* itself came to be used of anything nonsensical, impractical, or wholly unwarranted. By the mid-1800s, the expression had become so widely used that its spelling began to simplify; *Buncombe* morphed into *bunkum* and was eventually shorted into *bunk*. The opposite term *debunk* eventually emerged in 1923.

As the word itself changed, however, its connection to Buncombe County, North Carolina, was lost, and both it and Felix Walker's claim to fame were relegated to the footnotes of the dictionary. In Buncombe County itself, however, a roadside sign still commemorates Congressman Walker's contribution to the English language: "FELIX WALKER, Revolutionary officer member of Congress, 1817–23," it reads, "where in 'talking for Buncombe' (County), he gave new meaning to the word."

CHAPTER 18

FIRE BLANKET

To many people, asbestos will be forever associated with warning signs around old high school buildings, office towers, and dated apartment blocks. The fibrous, silicate material that has long been used as a fire-proofing insulation has now also been known to be toxic. But as much as it may sound like a modern invention, asbestos has a long and eventful history and has been in use by human beings for more than 5,000 years.

Archaeological evidence shows that even in the Stone Age and early Bronze Age, around 3,000BCE, humans in northern Europe were using asbestos in firing pottery, and utilized its bizarre fibrous structure to strengthen clay pots and other vessels. The Ancient Egyptians wove asbestos fibers into their clothes to improve their durability and even used it in the mummification of some of their pharaohs and dignitaries. The Ancient Greeks likewise used asbestos in their clothing, as well as noting and studying its bizarre flame-retardant properties, while the name *asbestos* itself (which means "unquenchable") was first given to it by the Roman historian and naturalist Pliny the Elder, as far back as in the 1st century

CE.

The Romans too, opened asbestos mines all across the Mediterranean, and it's often claimed that the workers in these mines—as well as their employers—were among the first people to note its toxicity to human health. (Reportedly, some Roman-era writers advised not buying or trading in slaves who had worked in asbestos mines, as they so quickly became ill.) The larger-scale mining of asbestos did not begin until much later, of course, and it was not until the 18th and 19th centuries that asbestos began to be produced industrially in any great quantity. It was even later—in fact, in the early 1900s—that the true extent of its negative effects on human health was finally described in any detail.

This extraordinary material has an equally extraordinary history. But perhaps the most bizarre chapter in this long history took place in the court of Charlemagne the Great, the first emperor of the Holy Roman Empire, more than a thousand years ago.

According to numerous contemporary accounts, Charlemagne—who ruled over Europe's Holy Roman Empire from 800–814 CE—had a tablecloth woven from asbestos, with which to impress and amaze his dinner guests.

By Charlemagne's time, the imperviousness and flame-retardant qualities of asbestos were well known: It is believed that some Christian pilgrims and clerics at the time would wear asbestos crosses, thinking their inflammableness proved they came from the true cross. For Charlemagne, however, these qualities were less of a chance to prove his religious devotion, and more a chance to wow his dinner guests.

Reportedly, Charlemagne would serve his guests a lavish banquet atop his asbestos tablecloth, and then once the plates, dishes, and goblets had all been cleared away, he would haul the cloth from the table and toss it into a fire in front of his presumably utterly bemused dining companions. The fire would burn off all the wine stains and spilled food from the surface of the cloth, of course, leaving only the unspoiled asbestos beneath it, utterly unharmed by the flames. The cloth could then be collected from the fire and thrown back over the table, ready to be used again.

Perhaps understandably, some of Charlemagne's guests are believed to have become concerned that the emperor's unburnable table cloth was the work of sorcery or black magic. Nowadays, of course, we know that it's just another bizarre chapter in the equally bizarre history of this remarkable substance!

CHAPTER 19

NAKED POWER

When you're the holder of the highest office in the land, finding the free time to indulge in a hobby or a pastime to relax and free up some headspace is usually easier said than done. But throughout history—from horse riding to basketball, from dog walking to golf—the Presidents of the United States have found all kinds of ways to wind down after a long day as Commander in Chief.

Of all the presidents and their pastimes, however, perhaps the strangest is that of John Quincy Adams. A former Massachusetts senator and his predecessor President James Monroe's Secretary of State, Adams was elected to office in 1825—becoming only the sixth president in US history and, as the eldest son of second president John Adams, the first relative of a former president to follow a family member into office.

Adams was reportedly a habitual early riser, writing in his diary in 1818 that, "I rise usually between four and five—walk two miles, bathe in Potomac River, and walk home, which occupies two hours." And after his election to office, Adams kept to this standard morning routine as closely as possible, waking at or just before dawn down to the banks of the Potomac River to swim.

Swimming isn't too bizarre a hobby, of course. However, skinny dipping arguably is.

According to several contemporary events and accounts — including one by legendary New York journalist Thurlow Weed - President Adams' daily swims in the Potomac would be carried out completely naked. ("Adams seemed as much at home in that element as on terra firma," Weed once wrote.) And, according to those same contemporary accounts, that predilection for being in the nude occasionally proved something of a problem!

The journalist Anne Royal allegedly once stumbled across President Adams enjoying his early morning constitutional and promptly took it upon herself to sit on his clothes, abandoned on the riverbank, and refused to move off them until the president had guaranteed her an interview. (Alas, it seems this tale at least — which is often claimed to have led to the first presidential interview with a female journalist in US history! — is likely apocryphal.)

On another occasion, Adams decided that he would not only take a dip in the water but would swim across the entire width of the Potomac, and so enlisted the help of a servant from the White House to row him across the river so that he could swim back. Midway over the river, however, the boat came into trouble and capsized, leaving Adams — who was already unclothed — to flounder his way back to the White House side of the river prematurely. As for the servant, he is said to have somehow managed to wriggle out of his heavy, waterlogged overcoat and trousers while in the water, for fear of them weighing him down, and likewise ended up washed up on the shore of the river beside the president, completely naked. Adams was left with little option but to give his clothes—which were still left on the shore—to the servant to wear so that he could run back to the White House and fetch him a new set before anyone noticed.

CHAPTER 20

FREEDOM OF SPEECH

With the occasional exception of the biggest awards of the night—as well as a few superlative winners, A-listers, or long overdue recognitions—nowadays Oscar speeches are now limited to just 45 seconds. After that time has elapsed, winners whose thank-you's threaten to last longer than the three-quarters of a minute cut-off point are gently played off the stage by music from the ceremony's in-house orchestra. Some winners, however, don't require quite so long to actually make their speech.

Despite being among cinema's greatest ever directors, Alfred Hitchcock memorably never won a competitive Oscar in his entire career, and had to make do instead with receiving the honorary Irving G Thalberg Memorial Award in 1968. You might think that after waiting several decades to be recognized by the Academy, Hitchcock would want to make the most of the occasion, but his speech lasted a grand total of six seconds: "Thank you," he said, before pausing and adding simply, "very much indeed."

Likewise, when Joe Pesci won the award for Best Supporting Actor for *Goodfellas* in 1991, he simply said, "It's my privilege, thank you." The director Delbert Mann, winner of the Best Director Oscar for *Marty* in 1956, simply exclaimed, "Thank you, thank you very much. Appreciate it." Actors Gloria Grahame, William Holden, and Patty Duke all likewise said a simple "thank you" when they approached the Oscar microphone before leaving the stage. And the legendary filmmaker Billy Wilder — whose movie *The Apartment* defeated Hitchcock's *Psycho* in 1961 — quipped, "Thank you so much, you lovely discerning people," when he picked up the award for Best Director.

But if those are among the Academy's shortest Oscar speeches, what about the longest? For that, we need to head back to the early 1940s.

The British–American actress Greer Garson was one of the biggest stars of the Golden Age of Hollywood, achieving an unprecedented five consecutive Best Actress nominations every year from 1941 to 1945. And it was for the second of these nominations, for her title role in the wartime drama *Mrs. Miniver*, that Garson won the Best Actress Oscar.

Making her way to the stage, Garson graciously collected her prize from fellow actress Joan Fontaine, approached the microphone on the podium, and began her speech with the words, "I'm practically unprepared." That may have been the case, but Garson certainly wasn't lost for things to say.

In her speech, she waxed lyrical on everything from the meaningful role of the Academy Awards in the wider filmmaking community, and what movie-making means as both an emerging and evolving art form, and as a medium of artistic expression. In all, she spoke for a total of almost six minutes—earning not just an Oscar, but a place in the *Guinness Book of Records* for the longest Oscar speech in movie history.

As gracious as Garson's speech was, however, it seems that its long-windedness did not go down too well with the members of the Academy (perhaps not least because hers was the last win of the evening, and she was delivering it to an exhausted audience at almost two o'clock in the morning). As a result, the Academy soon afterward introduced the three-quarters of a minute time-cap on winners' speeches. As for Garson, despite going on to secure another four Oscar nominations over the next two decades, she was never awarded a prize by the Academy again!

CHAPTER 21

LORD OF THE SINGS

Peter Jackson's epic movie adaptations of JRR Tolkien's *Lord of the Rings* stories are among the most popular, most successful, and most critically acclaimed films of the 21st century. Despite popular opinion, however, they are not the first movie adaptations of Tolkien's magnum opus.

In 1978, the controversial filmmaker and animator Ralph Bakshi, a former Terrytoons artist, whose career included working on such characters as Deputy Dawg, Mighty Mouse, and Spider-Man; adapted the first book-and-a-half of Tolkien's *Lord of the Rings* trilogy into a grand two-and-a-half-hour animated fantasy movie. Featuring the voices of numerous high-profile British stars (including John Hurt and *Star Wars'* star Anthony Daniels), the movie covered the events of Tolkien's *Fellowship of the Ring* and the first half of the second story, *The Two Towers*, but stopped short of completing the tale and so left the concluding events of *The Return of the King* untold. Nevertheless, the movie has since proved hugely popular with Tolkien fans and fanatics. It is now considered the earliest Tolkien adaptation ever to make its way onto the silver screen.

It was, however, very nearly the second.

In 1963, the Beatles signed a three-film deal with movie production company - United Artists. Their first film, the comedy mockumentary *A Hard Day's Night*, proved such a success that it was quickly followed by a second, *Help!*, that parodied the early James Bond movies and saw the band fight off the influences of a mysterious cult while traveling the world. Thwarted by production issues, *Help!*, was less well-received than its predecessor, and as the decade wore on — and the band itself began to drift apart, ahead of their breakup in 1970 — securing a third and final movie to complete their contract began to prove difficult.

1967's *Magical Mystery Tour* was made for television by the BBC, and so did not meet United Artists' contractual obligations. 1968's animated adventure *Yellow Submarine* likewise did not tick the right contractual boxes, as the Beatles did not appear on screen until the very end of the movie and had their voices in the animation recorded by actors. (John Lennon, for instance, was voiced by acclaimed English stage actor and future best-selling author John Clive, while Paul McCartney was voiced by comic actor and star of the popular sitcom *Keeping Up Appearances*, Geoffrey Hughes.) Clearly, to fulfill their obligations with United Artists, the Beatles needed a film in which they could all appear on screen, for the full length of the story — and by the end of the 1960s, they had set their sights on a truly epic saga.

The Beatles decided that their third and final movie with United Artists would be a psychedelic musical adaptation of Tolkien's *Lord of the Rings*, with Paul McCartney as Frodo,

Ringo as his sidekick Sam, George Harrison as the wise wizard Gandalf the Gray, and John Lennon as the monstrous and duplicitous Gollum. As if that weren't enough, the movie, the Beatles decided, would be directed by one of cinema's rising stars at the time: Stanley Kubrick.

Unfortunately (or fortunately, depending on what you might think!), this insanely extravagant project never truly got off the ground—not in the least because Kubrick himself quickly turned the idea down as soon as he was approached, claiming that the stories were too grand and ultimately unfilmable. Tolkien, too, wasn't too keen on the idea of having his greatest books adapted by a pop group and refused to grant the rights to the producers because he hated modern music. ("In a house three doors away dwells a member of a group of young men who are evidently aiming to turn themselves into a Beatle Group," Tolkien once wrote to a friend of his. "The noise is indescribable.")

With a director not keen to get involved, no negotiation over the movie rights forthcoming from Tolkien, and a band on the brink of splitting up, the Beatles' adaptation of the *Lord of the Rings* sadly never materialized. But there was, it appears, a silver lining.

When the first of Peter Jackson's films finally arrived in cinemas in 2001, Sir Paul McCartney himself approached the director to say that he was glad his and the other Beatles' movie had never made it to the cinema, as it would have made Jackson's adaptations unlikely ever to have been made. We may not have the Beatles' version of the stories, then, but we do at least have one.

CHAPTER 22

A NICE LITTLE EARNER

Anyone who enjoys a little a bit of antiquing, dreams of finding a genuine treasure hidden somewhere amidst the dusty knickknacks, rickety furniture, and other bric-a-brac that tends to fill most second-hand stores. It is certainly the case that some people are lucky enough to track down a real gem amidst the jumble—but few stories are as remarkable as the painting that was discovered at a Pennsylvania flea market in 1989.

The painting, a simple, somewhat dreary-looking landscape picture of some countryside by an artist whose signature was unreadable, was bought at a store in Adamstown by an anonymous buyer, who admitted he was more interested in its pretty gilt frame than the image inside it. He paid just $4 for it.

Some months later, when the time finally came to remove the painting from its frame so that it could be used elsewhere, the frame sadly splintered apart; but as it did so, a small folded document dropped out onto the floor, from between the canvas and the frame's wooden backboard. On closer inspection, the document turned out to be an original copy of the Declaration of Independence.

After the Declaration of Independence was signed on July 4, 1776, a local printer in Philadelphia named John Dunlap was hired to reproduce dozens more copies of the document. The plan was that these copies—which perhaps numbered as many as 200—could then be distributed to government and military leaders, and various towns and cities, right across the original 13 colonies, bringing news that America was now an independent nation.

The copy found behind the $4 painting was just the 24th of these original 1776 copies known to exist at the time. Unsure of just how remarkable a discovery it was, in 1991 the owner took it to Sotheby's auction house to have it appraised; it was valued at anywhere between $800,000 and $1 million. "Here was the most important single printed page in the world, in the most spectacularly beautiful condition," auctioneer David Redden, the vice president of Sotheby's, told the *LA Times* at the time. "The fact that it has been in the backing of the frame preserved it," he went on, describing the document; which evidence showed was folded while the ink was still wet, way back in 1776, as "unspeakably fresh."

The copy of the Declaration went up for sale at Sotheby's on June 4, 1991, and defied all expectations to sell for a staggering $2.42 million. Not a bad return on a $4 investment!

CHAPTER 23

THE BIG GIPPER

Long before former reality show star and real estate mogul Donald Trump became President of the United States, Ronald Reagan was the first to successfully transition from entertainer to leader of the free world. He served as president during the height of the Cold War when one wrong move by either the US or Soviet Union could've spelled the end for us all. Reagan carefully balanced diplomacy with a strong stance against communism and the Soviet Union to win the Cold War and leave office as one of the most popular and effective presidents since World War II.

But if it wasn't for plenty of hard work and a couple of lucky breaks, the world never would've heard of Ronald Reagan.

Ronald Reagan, or "Ronnie," as his second wife Nancy affectionately referred to him as, seemed to have pretty clear if not boring future ahead of him when he was growing up in the small town of Dixon, Illinois. He planned to attend college, get a job, and start a family. Then, a chance job as a radio announcer opened him up to a new world.

Reagan moved to Hollywood in 1937, and after starring in

several bit roles in some very unforgettable films, he used his name recognition to enter politics.

Most thought it was ridiculous for a former actor to run for office, but Ronnie didn't let the critics affect his decisions. In fact, instead of starting small, as some suggested, by running for a seat in the state House of Representatives, Reagan decided to go big and run for governor of California as a Republican in 1966. Needless to say, California was quite different at that time politically, so Reagan was able to win in a landslide.

Reagan served two terms as California's governor and just as he used the visibility of his acting career to propel him into the governor's mansion in Sacramento, he did the same thing to reach the Whitehouse.

After becoming president in 1980, Reagan was able to lay out his vision for revamping America. The US had been suffering a recession and was on the losing end of some Cold War battles, so a guy like Reagan was just what the country needed.

By 1984, the US economy had rebounded and America's traditional enemies had once more shown respect for the country.

The 1980s truly was the decade of Reagan, from the booming economy to the tough stance on communism, it could be felt everywhere. Americans in New York and Los Angeles found common ground with those in the Dakotas and Mississippi to work together toward common goals. Some people criticize the excess and superficiality of the 1980s, but there is little doubt that Americans were more unified and less antagonistic during the "decade of excess."

People didn't talk about red states and blue states during the 1980s. After all, just about every state voted for Reagan so it didn't matter!

CHAPTER 24

CRAZY FACTS 3

1. There are six known records of William Shakespeare's signature, and he spells his name differently in every single one.

2. A single strand of spaghetti is called a spaghetto.

3. The motto of Harry Potter's Hogwarts school is "Never tickle a sleeping dragon."

4. There is a private ATM in the basement of Buckingham Palace for the exclusive use of the royal family.

5. Owls have cone-shaped eyeballs.

6. The parking sign was invented for the 1924 Amsterdam Olympics.

7. St. Lucia is the only independent country in the world named after a woman.

8. Some 18th-century prisoners in Paris were permitted to go free so long as they agreed to move to Louisiana.

9. King William III of England was killed when his horse stumbled on a molehill.

10. Medical MRI scans have proved that the part of our brain that responsible for good judgment switches off when we look at someone we're in love with.

11. In 2015, a bulldog named Otto set a world record by skateboarding through the legs of a chain of 30 different people in Lima, Peru.

12. Charles Dickens once became so excited about hearing some good news while walking with a friend that he tried to dance with a random woman who happened to be walking by him. The woman recoiled in shock, fell over backward, and broke her arm.

13. Bats can catch more than 1,000 insects every hour.

14. Penguins whose eggs fail to hatch or whose chicks perish before adulthood have been known to kidnap other birds' chicks and rear them as their own.

15. On average by square mile, the United Kingdom experiences more tornados than any other country.

CHAPTER 25

POLLY MOUTH

From George Washington's American foxhound "Sweetlips" to the Obamas' pair of Portuguese water dogs, Bo and Sunny, the White House has a long history of presidential pets. In fact, of all the presidents in the more than 200-year history of the United States, only two have chosen not to take a pet into the White House: James K Polk in the 1840s and Donald Trump.

In that time, the White House has also been home to some somewhat peculiar animals. Although the tale may be apocryphal, John Quincy Adams reportedly kept a pet alligator in the East Room of the White House. Thomas Jefferson famously owned two brown bear cubs, which he was eventually compelled to donate to the Peale Museum in Philadelphia when they proved too dangerous to keep at home. Martin Van Buren was gifted two tiger cubs by the Sultan of Oman. Benjamin Harrison kept two opossums known as Mr. Reciprocity and Mr. Protection - names inspired by the 1896 Republican party slogan. Theodore Roosevelt owned a garter snake his daughter chose to name Emily Spinach. And Calvin Coolidge had a pygmy hippopotamus known as Billy - or, to give him his full name, "Mr. William

Johnson Hippopotamus."

Of all the presidents' pets, however, one of the most memorable was a Congo African grey parrot called Poll, or Polly, that was owned by President Andrew Jackson. What made Polly such a memorable addition to the presidency, moreover, had less to do with President Jackson's life, and more to do with what happened after his death.

Polly was reportedly originally President Jackson's wife Rachel's pet, but when she passed away of a heart attack very unexpectedly in December 1828—just days after her husband's election victory and a matter of weeks before his inauguration—Jackson adopted Polly as his own.

As president, Jackson was known for his no-nonsense attitude—a reputation that he had originally earned during his military service when the soldiers under his command had given him the nickname "Old Hickory" for his toughness and straightforwardness. And it seems at least some of that plain-speaking candor rubbed off on Polly, as before long she had amassed quite a rich vocabulary of curse words.

Alas, as well as being capable of mimicking their owners' somewhat fruity language, parrots are also known for their longevity. So when President Jackson himself passed away in Nashville 1845 at the age of 78, Polly was still going strong— having now outlived both of her former owners. As a result, Polly was brought along to her keeper's funeral, along with more than 1,000 guests and mourners gathered to celebrate the life of their former Commander in Chief.

Unfortunately, Polly didn't quite appreciate the reverence of the occasion, and shortly after President Jackson's funeral began, the bird started swearing very loudly and very raucously. "Before the sermon and while the crowd was gathering," recalled the funeral's cleric, the Reverend William Menefee Norment, in a later account, "a wicked parrot that was a household pet got excited, and commenced swearing so loud and long as to disturb the people." The bird, Norment explained, was apparently "excited by the multitude" of people in front of it and, as a result, "let loose perfect gusts of cuss words." People were "horrified and awed at the bird's lack of reverence," and eventually Polly "had to be carried from the house."

What happened to Polly after the shambolic funeral of President Jackson is unknown. But her indecent outbursts nevertheless earned her — and her equally uncompromising owner — a place in the history books.

CHAPTER 26

YOU'RE FIRED

The Great Fire of London of 1666 destroyed almost the entire Old City of London. The fire broke out in the early hours of Sunday morning, September 2, 1666, in the basement of a baker's shop in Pudding Lane owned by a gentleman named Thomas Farriner. Although Farriner initially claimed to have extinguished the fire in his bakery himself, it soon burned out of control, and with such ferocity and speed that it quickly proved all but impossible to hold back.

The fire went on to burn for more than three days, at which time more than 13,000 homes, some 87 churches, and more than 40 livery and trade halls across London were reduced to ashes. The original historic gates of the City of London were severely damaged, as too was the city's main Guildhall, the original St. Paul's Cathedral, and the Royal Exchange—in some instances, beyond all repairs. There was one silver lining, at least: Though accounts of the disaster vary, the human toll of the fire is alleged to have been relatively small. Within a few years of the blaze, the English writer Edward Chamberlayne explained that while much of the city was destroyed, "not above six or eight persons were burnt."

There was, however, at least one death that could be indirectly attributed to the fire—namely, that of a bizarre and tragic character that was executed in the aftermath of the blaze for having claimed to have started it.

Born in Rouen, in northern France, in 1640, Robert Hubert was a watchmaker by trade. Although details of his life are sketchy at best, Hubert is believed to have spent much of his adult life living and working in London, although he spoke little English and likely divided much of his time between Britain and the Continent. Indeed, on the night that the Great Fire of London first broke out, Hubert was not even in England but instead on board the *Maid of Stockholm*, a North Sea ferry that had been traveling between Sweden—where Hubert had reportedly been visiting relatives—and his native France.

At the time of the fire, England was engaged in the Second Anglo-Dutch War, a bitter and long-lasting conflict with the Kingdom of the Netherlands. Ultimately, any non-English vessel (or, for that matter, any non-English national) that happened to stray into English waters was viewed with considerable suspicion. As a result, the *Maid of Stockholm* was intercepted on August 31 on its return journey back across the North Sea from Sweden, and forcibly redirected to London. There, its passengers and crew would have to remain in limbo, awaiting permission from the city's authorities to continue their journey on to France. They arrived in London on September 3 to find the entire city ablaze.

All of those on board the ship—including its captain, known only as a Mr. Peterson—stood on the deck of the ship watching helplessly as the disaster unfolded before their eyes. And it was there that Captain Peterson reportedly overheard Robert Hubert muttering softly and repeatedly to himself the words, "Very well, very well! Yes, yes!" As he watched the city being burned to the ground. Hubert's behavior proved disconcerting, and with the cause of the fire at that time unclear—and with an air of suspicion already rife in the city due to the ongoing war—Peterson became concerned that Hubert may be a spy, a traitor, or else in some way involved in the city's destruction.

Later accounts of Hubert's life and personality have suggested that he may have suffered from some sort of mental illness, or perhaps even a condition similar to what would be known as Tourette's Syndrome today. That would certainly explain his seemingly unconscious muttering on the deck of the *Maid of Stockholm*, and why Captain Peterson might have become so unnerved by his behavior. Either way, Hubert's mumbling proved upsetting enough to see him thrown below deck and imprisoned in the hold of the *Maid of Stockholm* on Captain Peterson's orders. Early the following morning, however, Hubert somehow managed to escape the ship's hold and fled onto the Thames dockside by jumping down from a small hatch window in the captain's quarters. Captain Peterson himself later testified that he saw Hubert flee along the quayside, and vanish into a crowd.

When news of Hubert's curious behavior and clandestine escape from the *Maid of Stockholm* became known, the London authorities soon presumed that he must have somehow been involved in the fire. A week later, on September 11, 1666, he was arrested in Romford, a town around 12 miles east of the city of London, and taken into custody. Precisely what happened to him while he was under arrest remains unclear, but by the time Hubert appeared in court in London several days later, a strange and wholly inconsistent confession had been extracted from him.

According to Huber's testimony, he claimed to have started the fire by throwing a makeshift grenade through a window in Thomas Farriner's bakery. The fact that the fire broke out two days before Hubert and the *Maid of Stockholm* even arrived in the city was paid little heed—as was the fact that Thomas Farriner's bakery had no windows through which a grenade could be thrown. Nevertheless, despite the obvious holes in Hubert's testimony, his confession sealed his fate: the court had their scapegoat, and Hubert was sentenced to death. On October 27, 1666, he was taken out to the Tyburn gallows in London and hanged. And with that, the Great Fire of London had claimed its final victim—nearly two months after it had been extinguished.

CHAPTER 27

A ROAR DEAL

When the Metro-Goldwyn-Mayer movie production company was founded in 1924, the company needed to adopt an emblem to convey to the rest of Hollywood that a new movie-making force to be reckoned with had arrived. Turning to in-house designer Howard Dietz for inspiration, MGM opted to choose a roaring lion as their logo—partly because of the message that the king of the beasts would send out (and partly as a tribute to the Lions athletics team of Dietz's alma mater, Columbia University).

Over the century or so since then, a total of seven different lions have acted as the centerpiece of MGM's famous "roaring lion" logo. The very first was a creature named Slats, but unlike all those who followed him, Slats did not roar. Instead, in his "bumper" (that is, the short, few-seconds-long clip that rolls before a movie, advertising the studio who made it) Slats merely stared out imperiously around the audience. The reason Slats did not roar? He only appeared in MGM's earliest silent movies.

After the dawn of sound and color pictures in the 1920s and 30s, MGM decided that their logo needed updating, and so adopted a new lion named Jackie. His roar was recorded using in a gramophone, inside a specially-constructed soundstage built around his cage on the MGM lot. Footage of Jackie roaring was also recorded, and he plus his roar made their debut on MGM's first sound feature, *White Shadows in the South Seas*, in 1928. A decade later, he made his Technicolor debut before 1939's *The Wizard of Oz*.

Jackie remained the official MGM lion right through to 1956, although a handful of others—named Telly, Coffee, Tanner, and George—were used intermittently on various other pictures from the 1930s through to the late 1950s. For almost every MGM picture since 1957, the MGM lion has been Leo— a captive-bred lion, born in Dublin Zoo, Ireland, who as well as becoming the logo of MGM also appeared on screen in a handful of pictures in the 50s and 60s. It was Leo the Lion, too, who in 1959 made an unexpected entry in Hollywood history.

While Slats the Lion was kept intentionally silent for the soundless movies of the 1920s, every other MGM lion since then has roared before an MGM film. But when biblical epic *Ben-Hur* finally made its way to the silver screen in 1959, the MGM lion was—for the first time in more than three decades—once again kept deliberately silent.

Quite why Leo the Lion was silenced before 1959's *Ben-Hur* has been the subject of numerous theories and over the years. Some people claim that it was a protest to the end of the McCarthyism era of Hollywood suspicion and censorship, while others like to think that it was an in-joke—a knowing callback to MGM's original 1925 adaptation of the *Ben-Hur* story, which had, like all of the studio's earliest movies, been a silent film. The real reason that Leo was silenced before the 1959 film was a lot more straightforward than either of those.

Given its biblical setting and religious context, *Ben-Hur* opens with a simple recreation of the nativity. Reportedly, director William Wyler (who would go on to win the Academy Award for Best Director for *Ben-Hur* the following year) thought that preceding that serene opening scene with the rousing roar of Leo the lion wouldn't quite set the right mood. And so, fearing that this opening scene might otherwise feel out of place, he requested that for the first and only time since the silent era, the MGM lion be silenced.

CHAPTER 28

PUTIN ON A SHOW

If there's one thing that Russian leader Vladimir Putin likes to prove and propagandize about, it's his macho reputation.

Over the many years of his premiership in Russia, President Putin has taken part in many publicity stunts and set pieces, all in the hope of cultivating a certain masculine image in the Russian media, and among the Russian people.

Among President Putin's many attempts to bolster this macho image, he has been recorded tracking polar bears in Siberia; driving a Formula One car around the St. Petersburg race track; sailing a submersible through an Arctic shipwreck; shooting a skin-sampling harpoon into the back of a whale from a zoological research vessel; catching and reeling in a 46-pound pike while on a fishing trip to Siberia; and discovering a cache of lost Ancient Greek pots while diving off Russia's Black Sea coast.

Quite how genuine these bizarre feats and stunts are have been the source of considerable speculation over the years — and the Russian media has on at least one occasion been forced to issue a retraction when some of President Putin's achievements have genuinely proved to be too unbelievable to be true. (Those Ancient Greek vessels he found in the Black Sea, for instance, were later grudgingly revealed to have been planted at the bottom of the sea for President Putin to "discover.") But there is at least one field in which Putin is truly as capable as he and his media purport him to be.

He's so good at it, that he's even starred in his own instructional video.

Long before becoming President, in 1975 Putin joined the Soviet secret police force, the KGB, and undertook his early training at a KGB school in his home city of Leningrad. It was there that he first began to learn and study martial arts, beginning with a traditional Russian martial art named Sambo, and eventually moving on to judo, in which he was awarded a "Master of Sports" title in the late 1970s. President Putin has since gone on to claim that judo is his favorite sport — so much so that, in 2004, he co-authored an instructional book about judo, published in Russia under the title *Judo with Vladimir Putin*. The same book was later released to English-speaking markets as *Judo: A History, Theory, and Practice*, and in October 2008 was adapted into an 82-minute instructional video.

Entitled *Let's Learn Judo with Vladimir Putin*, the film was released — amid considerable publicity in Russia — to coincide with President Putin's 56th birthday celebrations. The president, dressed in a full judo uniform, announced the video at a press conference in Moscow, before demonstrating several of his favorite moves to an expectant crowd of journalists. "In a bout, compromises and concessions are permissible," Putin advises in the video, "but only in one case: if it is for victory."

As bizarre as the Russian president's instructional judo

movie may be, however, within the judo community it was nevertheless seemingly well-received: In 2012, President Putin was officially promoted to the Eighth Dan (out of the ten official 'dan' or fighting levels of professional judo) by the International Judo Federation.

CHAPTER 29

DON'T BET ON IT

In a career spanning several decades, the American humorist, writer, and publisher Bennett Cerf, well-known to millions of Americans in the 1950s and 60s for his numerous appearances on panel show *What's My Line;* was also one of the co-founders of the worldwide publishing company Random House. During his many years with the company, Cerf worked with some of the 20th century's most acclaimed authors, including the likes of William Faulkner, Sinclair Lewis, Eugene O'Neill, and Robert Graves.

But Cerf later admitted that he considered only one of the authors on his company's books to be a true literary genius: Dr. Seuss.

Dr. Seuss - the pen name of children's author and poet Theodor Seuss "Ted" Geisel, wrote and illustrated more than 60 books for children in a career spanning six decades, including such instantly familiar titles as *If I Ran the Zoo* (1950), *Horton Hears a Who!* (1955), *The Cat in the Hat* (1957), and *How the Grinch Stole Christmas!* (1957). His unique sing-song writing style, crazy plotlines, and his equally bizarre and instantly recognizable drawing style all conspired to prove hugely popular with readers and their parents alike. Today Seuss is considered one of the most successful children's authors of all time; his books have sold more than 600 million copies in more than 20 different languages worldwide.

But of all of his books and their madcap plotlines, at least one is matched by an equally bizarre story explaining how Dr. Seuss came to write it in the first place.

Dr. Seuss wrote one of his most famous titles, *The Cat In The Hat*, in response to a plea from schoolbook publisher at Houghton Mifflin to write a primer for early learners of English that was more exciting and more complex than traditional (and increasingly ineffective) primers like the *Dick and Jane* stories. A lucrative deal—in which Houghton Mifflin would publish an education edition to US schools, while Random House would produce a trade edition for sale in bookstores, was drawn up, and *The Cat In The Hat* arrived in schools and stores across the United States in 1957. It proved an almost immediate success, selling more than 12,000 copies every month in the early years of its release—and as a result, Random House was soon keen to try to repeat its success.

In discussing what Dr. Seuss' next title could be, publisher Bennett Cerf happened to note that, as a children's literary primer, *The Cat In The Hat* had a total vocabulary of just over 200 different words. This seemed a remarkable achievement and led to Cerf considering whether this figure could be improved upon. As a result, he offered Dr. Seuss a wager: Cerf bet that Dr. Seuss could not write a new children's book limited to a total vocabulary of just 50 different words or less. Dr. Seuss happily accepted the wager; and, it's fair to say, more than rose to the occasion.

The book that was the result of this curious wager was the children's classic, *Green Eggs and Ham*, which was published by Random House in 1960. In its entirety, *Green Eggs and Ham* is written using nothing more than the 50 different words *a, am, and, anywhere, are, be, boat, box, car, could, dark, do, eat, eggs, fox, goat, good, green, ham, here, house, I, if, in, let, like, may, me, mouse, not, on, or, rain, Sam, say, see, so, thank, that, the, them, there, they, train, tree, try, will, with, would* and *you*. No other word appears in the entire text of the book.

Although Cerf had quite decisively lost his bet with Dr. Seuss, there was, at least, a silver lining for him though: Despite its limited vocabulary, *Green Eggs and Ham* proved even more successful than its predecessor and went on to sell more than eight million copies worldwide.

CHAPTER 30

A PHARAOH'LD TIME

When Queen Elizabeth II celebrated her diamond jubilee in 2012—marking a record-setting 60 years on the British throne—the UK and the Commonwealth erupted into a vast series of flag-strewn tea parties, colorful villages fetes, and Union Jack street parades. That might be how royal anniversaries are celebrated today, but journey back through history and the celebrations surrounding royal jubilees grow a little more unusual. And if you go far enough back in time—to the very earliest days of Ancient Egypt, in fact—then royal jubilees become very unusual indeed.

More than 5,000 years ago in Ancient Egypt, after a pharaoh had ruled over their kingdom for 30 years, the Egyptians observed a bizarre ritual called Heb-Sed.

The Heb-Sed Festival, or the Sed Jubilee as it is also known, was one of the oldest and longest-running rituals in Ancient Egyptian history. Records of it taking place have been unearthed dating from as far back as 3,000 BCE, and it is known to have continued to take place long into the Roman Empire's conquest of Egypt in the 1st century BCE.

Although accounts of it are hazy and lost in time, Heb-Sed is believed to have been a fairly prolonged affair, often including numerous different stages and ceremonies in which the pharaoh would perform all kinds of ritualistic activities; from visiting temples to make offerings to the gods, to symbolically firing arrows towards the four corners of their kingdom, and being repeatedly crowned and re-crowned, in a range of contexts and locations. The precise content of the festival, however, was often left up to the pharaoh themselves, which ensured that no Heb-Sed was ever the same as any other. But each one always tended to take place during the month of Koiak—the fourth month of the Egyptian calendar, equivalent to what is now November, in the pharaoh's jubilee year, coinciding with the annual flooding of the Nile. And what's more, each year's Heb-Sed always culminated in one of history's most bizarre spectacles.

After all the preceding rituals and ceremonies had been carried out, the pharaoh would typically return to their grandest and largest palace. There, they would change into an extraordinary costume comprising a short kilt-like garment worn around the waist, with the tail of a bull or some similar creature attached to the back of it; and then be made to sprint around a specially constructed running track drawn up in the courtyard of their palace, cheered on by a large crowd of subjects, and observed by an audience of dignitaries and high priests.

Perhaps understandably, Egyptologists aren't entirely clear as to the meaning of this strange footrace . Likely, it was originally intended as nothing more than a show of strength; a chance for the pharaoh to demonstrate their vitality and athleticism, and thereby prove their fitness and ability to continue reigning over their kingdom. (Indeed, the name *Heb-Sed* itself commemorates a jackal-headed deity believed to be related to the Egyptian god of power and war, which might imply that this ritual *was* intended as a demonstration of strength or vigor.)

Another theory, however, claims that the race was purely ceremonial or symbolic, and was merely meant to represent the pharaoh outrunning their old age. Another contention is that the race was intended to represent the pharaoh reaching out to all the corners of their kingdom, much like the arrows shot into the direction of Egypt's four corners. Yet another suggestion is that the Heb-Sed race may have had a much more practical use. Perhaps if the pharaoh were not able to complete the course, then they were deemed no longer fit enough to rule and would be promptly sacrificed, to make way for a younger, more vigorous successor. Whatever its purpose, once a pharaoh had celebrated their first Heb-Sed — in the 30th year of their rule — they were expected to repeat the process every three years thereafter, right up until their death.

Whatever the meaning of the Heb-Sed ceremony was, there's no doubt that it took place. Countless images of the kings and queens of Egypt running their Heb-Sed footrace have been found in documents and inscriptions over the decades, as have the makeshift royal running tracks themselves. The great step-pyramid of the pharaoh Djoser at Saqqara in northeast Egypt has an entire courtyard set aside for the king's Heb-Sed course, dating back to more than 2,600 years BCE.

CHAPTER 31

TICKET TO STRIDE

On the morning of January 28, 1896, a landmark in the history of transport was made — albeit by an unsuspecting local police constable, in the sleepy English village of Paddock Wood in Kent, 40 miles outside London.

As he cycled his usual route through the village, the unnamed constable's normal morning routine was suddenly shattered by the sight and sound of an early Benz motor car tearing its way through the local neighborhood at a heady 8mph. That speed might not sound all too impressive these days, but at the time in England, the legal speed limit for motorized vehicles on English roads was just 2mph — meaning the driver of the car in question was behaving extraordinarily recklessly.

As a result, the police constable took up the chase, and for the next five miles, he remained in pursuit of the car on his bicycle, as it trundled its way through the winding country roads of Paddock Wood and the surrounding countryside. Eventually, the driver, a gentleman named Walter Arnold, stopped his car, and the exhausted constable was finally able to issue him with the very first speeding ticket in the history of motorized transport.

The story proved something of a sensation in late Victorian England, with the *London Daily News* reporting that Mr. Arnold and his "horseless carriage" were to be charged on four separate counts: driving a "locomotive without a horse"; having fewer than three people in charge of his horseless locomotive; failing to have his name and address inscribed somewhere on the chassis of the vehicle; and, lastly, the speeding fine itself - breaking the legal limit more than fourfold.

At his trial at Royal Tunbridge Wells in Kent a few days later, Arnold's defense team put forward the case that the laws at that time were based on horse-drawn carriages, locomotives, and other increasingly outdated modes of transport. Arnold's motorcar, they argued, could not and should not be subject to the same rules. Unfortunately, the court disagreed, and Arnold was fined 5 shillings - plus £2 and 11 pence costs - for "using a carriage without a locomotive horse," equivalent to around £200 ($260) today.

On each of the other three charges, he was fined 1 shilling plus 9 shillings costs (equivalent to £45/$60 today). In summing up, the court explained that Arnold could have avoided at least one of the punitive charges put against him if he had followed the rules of the road at the time and safely driven his car with someone walking ahead of it waving a red warning flag.

The entire debacle may have ended up costing Mr. Arnold the equivalent of over $400, but it seems that the trial itself, and the media buzz that surrounded it, may have proved something of a boon for him. Arnold was one of England's earliest motorcar dealers, responsible for importing new Benz models from mainland Europe. The commotion surrounding his case, ultimately, might have proved to be useful publicity for his business, with interest in motorized transport already growing at the end of the 19th century.

It's also likely that the case helped to modernize the laws surrounding motor vehicles, which went on to be redrawn by the end of the year. From 1897 onwards, it was officially deemed no longer necessary to have at least three people in charge of a single moving vehicle at any one time. Nor was it necessary any longer to have a flag bearer walk in front of your car as you drove it. The speed limit on England's roads, meanwhile, was eventually raised from a somewhat restrictive 2mph to a mind-boggling 14mph. It seems Arnold's speeding ticket proved a landmark in more ways than one!

CHAPTER 32

CRAZY FACTS 4

1. Alfred Hitchcock was terrified of eggs. "I'm frightened of eggs," he once told an interviewer. "That white round thing without any holes … Have you ever seen anything more revolting than an egg yolk breaking and spilling its yellow liquid?"

2. The movie *Die Hard 2* was released in Hungary under the title *Your Life is More Expensive*.

3. William Shakespeare's father was the official ale-taster of Stratford upon Avon. One of the tests he administered to ensure the quality of the city's ale remained high was to sit in a pool of beer in leather trousers and see how sticky the beer became as it warmed up.

4. Rats can be trained to play hide and seek, and appear to celebrate when they are found.

5. Since humans started feeding garden birds, some species have been found to have evolved longer bills to access bird feeders.

6. Expectant mothers' feet typically increase by half a shoe size during pregnancy. Often, they never return to their

original size.

7. England's Oxford University is older than the Aztec Empire.

8. There are no trees and no rivers on the entire island of Malta.

9. The currency of Botswana, the pula, takes its name from a local word meaning "rain." The name is used because rain in Botswana, like money in general, is so difficult to come by, yet so important to the country's economy.

10. On average, one ostrich egg contains the same amount of liquid as 24 hen's eggs.

11. It became standard practice to add the milk to a cup of tea first because early teacups were often brittle and liable to shatter when boiling water was poured directly into them.

12. 12,345,679 multiplied by the missing number in the sequence, 8, is equal to 98,765,432.

13. The Breeches Bible was a 1579 edition of the Bible that included a passage that described Adam and Eve sewing fig leaves together to make trousers to hide their shame.

14. Tug of war was contested as an official sport at every Summer Olympic Games from 1900 to 1920.

15. No one knows why the alphabet is in the order that it is in.

CHAPTER 33

THE HISTORY BOOKS

In 1941, the American author JD Salinger submitted a number of his early short stories to the *New Yorker* magazine. Despite having had some success writing for similar publications, including *Story* and *Collier's* magazine, the *New Yorker* proved a tougher publication to crack, and the magazine initially turned many of Salinger's stories down. Finally, however, in December 1941, the editors agreed to publish a story he had written entitled *Slight Rebellion off Madison*, a tale about a disaffected teenager in Manhattan named Holden Caulfield, dealing with the events of his adolescence, and set in the run-up to World War II.

Acceptance by one of America's foremost and widely-read magazines proved a huge boost of confidence for Salinger's burgeoning writing career, and it's fair to say he was overjoyed. But only a few weeks later, Japan attacked the US military post at Pearl Harbor, and the United States was drawn into World War II. The wartime context of Salinger's story suddenly now proved problematic, and the *New Yorker* had little option but to pull it from their next publication.

Understandably, Salinger was devastated, but he also had

little time to recover his thoughts, and resubmit his work. Just a few months later, the 23-year-old was drafted into the US Army and arrived in Europe in the spring of 1942 as part of the 12th Infantry Regiment, 4th Infantry Division.

In the months (and eventually years) that followed, Salinger was promoted to sergeant and assigned to a counter-intelligence unit known as "The Ritchie Boys" (after the military camp in Maryland where they were trained). The unit utilized Salinger's ability to speak both French and German, by having him interrogate Nazi prisoners of war and French resistance leaders. And throughout the entire time, Salinger used any free time he could muster to continue writing.

Incredibly, Salinger had arrived in Europe with draft copies of six short stories in his possession, and throughout his military service, he continued to hone and flesh out his writing and his characters as best he could in between bouts of training, duty, and combat. Eventually, he decided to combine multiple elements from all six tales into one single, longer story, and the teenage protagonist of *Slight Rebellion off Madison* — that original short story the *New Yorker* had turned down, then ultimately became the central character in his novella.

By the summer of 1944, the war in Europe was accelerating towards its bloody climax. On July 6, Salinger found himself drafted into the first wave of the Normandy Landings, scheduled to land on Utah Beach at 6:30 a.m. Eyewitness accounts claim Salinger's unit was delayed slightly, however, meaning that he likely landed amid the second wave of troops around 10-15 minutes later. But the delay proved a fortunate one.

Sea currents in the English Channel disrupted the earliest

Utah landings, and cast Salinger's boat almost 2,000 yards further south than planned, down to a quieter, less marshy part of the French coastline, away from the most heavily defended German outposts. An hour after landing, Salinger was marching westwards as part of a military convoy with some fellow troops, aiming to reconnect with other Allied military units further inland. And still, throughout it all, he carried his precious manuscripts with him. The first drafts of *The Catcher in the Rye*, now one of the greatest novels of the 20th century, had somehow survived the D-Day landings.

Just when this story cannot get any more unusual, two months later, on August 25, 1944, the Germans surrendered control of Paris. Salinger's counter-intelligence unit was posted to the French capital to root out Nazi collaborators among the residents. Incredibly, this posting allowed for what must surely be one of the most remarkable of chance meetings in literary history.

Salinger had an inkling that the great author and journalist Ernest Hemingway was, at that time, living in Paris as the war correspondent of *Collier's* magazine. And he also knew, if the rumor were true, precisely where Mr. Hemmingway would be.

In a brief break in his military service, Salinger hopped in a jeep and drove to the Ritz Hotel, and there requested a meeting with the great author. Hemingway was indeed housed at the Ritz and gratefully accepted Salinger's invitation; to his amazement, Hemmingway was already very familiar with Salinger's writing for *Collier's* and greeted him at the hotel as if he were an old friend. The two men found time to talk writing, literature, journalism, politics, and the ongoing course of the war before Salinger grew short on time and had to return to his barracks.

As the war raged on, Salinger would go on to fight in the Battle of the Bulge and the bloody Battle of Hürtgen Forest on the Western Front that rumbled on from September to December of 1944. (To this day, Hürtgen Forest remains the longest single battle in which the US military has ever been engaged.) But when the fighting was finally over the following year, Salinger opted to remain in Europe for a short time, to work on an Allied initiative of "Denazification," aimed at liberating concentration camps plus restoring peace and democracy to the German nation. He did not return to the US until 1946 when his writing career at last began to take shape.

The *New Yorker* belatedly published *Slight Rebellion off Madison* in the December of 1946, and, boosted by the publication of a second story, titled *A Perfect Day for Bananafish*, in 1948, Salinger finally began working on completing the novel he had envisaged while in Europe. *The Catcher in the Rye* went on to be published in 1951. Considered a generation-defining book, it has now sold more than 65 million copies worldwide.

CHAPTER 34

SEA SICKNESS

The line of succession to the British throne dates back more than 1,000 years. In that long history, countless wars, battles, coups, and conquests have seen the throne change hands between rivaling parties on numerous occasions. But on at least one of those, in the winter of 1120 CE, the entire English line of succession was altered forever by a series of events a lot more peculiar than any of those.

At that time, England was still under the control of the Norman rulers of northern France. The Norman Conquest of 1066 had seen William, the Duke of Normandy, defeat England's King Harold II at the Battle of Hastings. In doing so, William had taken control of Harold's kingdom as the newly-crowned King William I of England.

The entire Norman kingdom was now divided between the northern half of France and the southern half of Great Britain. And lying between the two of them was the English Channel.

That fractured setup meant that the English kings of the Norman era were often obliged to divide their time between the French and English halves of their kingdom, and therefore were compelled cross the English Channel countless times a year. So, on November 25, 1120, a vessel called *La Blanche-Nef* (literally the "White Ship") was chartered to carry the present English king, Henry I, the fourth surviving son of William the Conqueror, back across the Channel from France to England, along with all of the closest members of his court, much of his family, and his royal retinue.

At the last moment, however, Henry's travel plans were changed. A separate vessel was chartered for the King to travel on alone, while much of the rest of his family and his court were left to travel aboard the *White Ship*. Precisely what happened next is unclear, but as the afternoon drifted into the evening, it seems likely that the aggravating delay to the *White Ship*'s departure caused by the King's last-minute change of plans, or, perhaps, the freedom that came from no longer traveling under the King's watchful gaze, led the 300 or so passengers on board the *White Ship* to organize an impromptu party. Casks of wine and ale were ordered and brought onto the ship in huge quantities so that, by the time the *White Ship* was finally ready to depart that night, most of its passengers and crew were by now roaring drunk.

Amid all of this revelry, the *White Ship*'s captain, Thomas Fitz-Stephen, was challenged by some of his passengers to race the King's ship back to England. Knowing that his ship was indeed faster than one on which the King was now traveling, Fitz-Stephen accepted the challenge and set sail from the Norman port of Barfleur as quickly as possible. Within minutes of its departure, however, the *White Ship* came into trouble.

In the darkness of the winter night, the *White Ship* struck a submerged rock on her port side and quickly began to take on water. Just off the coast of Barfleur, the vessel suddenly capsized, throwing all of its passengers and crew into the freezing cold sea. The King's son and immediate heir, Prince William Adelin, was hauled from the water by unknown rescuers and lifted onto a small skiff (essentially a lifeboat). The skiff began to head back to the shore, ferrying the next in line to the throne to safety—but when William heard his sister, Princess Mathilde, crying out in the darkness, he selflessly ordered the skiff to turn back towards the wreck, in an attempt to save her.

There were so many desperate people clinging to the wreck of the *White Ship*, however, that William's lifeboat was soon swamped and dragged beneath the waves. So as the *White Ship* went down, so too did its passengers' one and only chance of rescue; both Prince William and Princess Mathilde were never seen again. Indeed, according to some reports from the time, there was just one survivor of the *White Ship* disaster: a butcher from Rouen, recorded only as M Berold, who managed to cling all night to a shattered piece of the ship's mast, while a thick fur overcoat he was wearing shielded him from the winter cold. He was found just after daybreak the following morning by a boat of local fishermen and taken back to the shore to recover.

Back in England, when news of the disaster reached King Henry, he was distraught. Almost all of his court, his closest friends and advisors, and his immediate family, including his heir, had all perished on board the *White Ship*. Ultimately, he was forced to name his only surviving legitimate child, his second daughter, Matilda, as his rightful successor. But the King's choice was to prove an unpopular one.

Despite originally swearing an oath to the King to accept Matilda's claim to the throne, on Henry's death in 1135, the Barons of England promptly reneged on their agreement. England had never before been ruled by a queen alone, and, what's more, Matilda's husband Geoffrey V of Anjou, the founder of the Plantagenet dynasty, was considered by the Barons to be an enemy to England.

Instead, the Barons supported a rival claim to the throne by Stephen of Blois, the Count of Boulogne, who was one of Henry I's nephews and a cousin of Matilda. For the next 18 years, the pair of rivals clashed repeatedly in a brutal fight to secure the throne, until Stephen proved victorious. He ruled as King of England until his death in 1154.

The rivalry between Stephen and Matilda (whom many consider the rightful heir) altered the course of the English line of succession. But, according to one account of the *White Ship* disaster, the entire affair only took place thanks to the most bizarre of circumstances back on that fateful night.

As one of the King's nephews, it later emerged that Stephen too had been due to travel to England aboard the *White Ship* alongside many of the other members of his family. As the drinks were served to the waiting passengers, however, Stephen quickly fell ill (possibly due to imbibing a spoiled cask of ale) and was forced to leave the ship with a debilitating bout of diarrhea. His upset stomach, however, was to prove his salvation. Stephen left the ship, escaped the entire *White Ship* disaster, and survived to launch his claim to the throne 15 years later. The course of English history and England's line of succession, ultimately, was altered beyond measure by nothing more than a queasy bout of seasickness!

CHAPTER 35

THE GREAT GADSBY

E is the most frequently used letter in the English language. Although estimates vary as to just how common it is, you can expect the letter E to account for around one in every nine letters you will read or write in an English text on average. (Contrast that to poor old Q, which only pops up once in every 500!)

Given E's status of commonness, some remarkably inventive poets and writers have enjoyed challenging themselves over the years, by attempting to come up with various works of poetry and literature that deliberately avoid using the letter E. And of all of these E-less works of literature, probably the most famous is a bizarre novel called *Gadsby*.

Published in November 1939, *Gadsby* was written over six months by the American author Ernest Vincent Wright. Apart from the author's name on the cover, a brief introduction, and a final concluding note, not a single one of the 50,000 words in Wright's novel contains a single letter E.

If you think that that sounds all but impossible, you'd be right. Wright even acknowledged as much, by claiming in his book that many of his friends believed that what he was trying to do was entirely unmanageable. ("All right," Wright proudly explains in the introduction, "the impossible has been accomplished.")

Of course, if you think that excluding, on average, one in every nine of the words in the English language might lead to some fairly bizarre prose, then you'd be right there too. When a wedding ceremony takes place in the story, for instance, Wright is forced to describe it as "a grand church ritual" to avoid the E's in words like *wedding* or *ceremony* — or, for that matter, words like *bride, bridesmaid, congregation,* and *guests*!

To ensure that he never once broke his own extraordinary self-imposed restriction, Wright taped down the E key of the typewriter on which he wrote his story. And to excuse the bizarre, verbose language he was forced to use in his book, Wright cleverly created a narrator for his tale who openly acknowledges his own bizarre way of talking, and accounts for it as nothing more than proof of his poor command of English. In that context, curious phrasings like a "grand church ritual" suddenly do not seem quite so bizarre.

Sadly, Wright never lived to see the success and the bizarre glory that his remarkable novel would go on to achieve. He died on October 7, 1939, just one month before *Gadsby* was finally published. Nevertheless, he is now considered one of a remarkable set of writers and authors who have written some of literature's most peculiar constrained works — some of which date back over many centuries.

The 4th -century Greek poet and writer Tryphiodorus, for example, rewrote Homer's epic tale the *Odyssey* as a series of

24 short books, each one excluding a different letter of the Greek alphabet. A Spanish renaissance playwright named Lope De Vega Carpio likewise wrote a series of five novels in the late 1500s and early 1600s, each of which omitted a different one of the five core vowels, A, E, I, O, and U. And in 1972, the French writer Georges Perec wrote a novella entitled *Les Revenentes*, that excluded every vowel *except* the letter E. *Les Revenentes*, ultimately, is essentially the direct opposite to Ernest Wright's *Gadsby*!

CHAPTER 36

THE DISAPPEARING PRINCE

On June 11, 1557, the long-reigning king of Portugal, John III, a grandson of Ferdinand and Isabella of Castile, the financiers of Christopher Columbus' transatlantic crossing, died suddenly at the age of 55. John's son and heir, also called John, had died three years earlier aged just 16, and as a result, the Portuguese throne passed on to John III's eldest grandson, Dom Sebastião. He became King Sebastian I of Portugal, at the age of just 3.

A 3-year-old king, of course, has somewhat limited powers of governance. So, for much of his childhood and the early years of his reign, Sebastian's role was taken over by his mother, Princess Joanna of Austria, King John III's daughter-in-law. A patient, intelligent, and astute leader, Joanna and her court acted as regent on behalf of Sebastian until he was old enough to rule on his own. In that time, she established a strong and successful period in Portugal's history, which saw the country flourish both domestically and internationally with the growth of its colonies and trade posts in Africa, India, and the Far East.

But in 1578, the now 24-year-old King Sebastian risked all of his mother and his court's hard work by embarking on a risky crusade in Northern Africa.

The position of the rightful Moroccan ruler, Sultan Abdallah Mohammed — a long-time ally of the Kingdom of Portugal, was being threatened by Abdallah's Turkish uncle, Mulay Abdelmalek. The sultan fled to Portugal in the summer of 1577 to request the assistance of King Sebastian and, ignoring all the best counsel of his teams of advisors, Sebastian agreed to assist. The following year, he raised an army and headed across the Straits of Gibraltar to North Africa.

In Morocco, Sebastian and his forces rejoined Sultan Abdallah Mohammed and his army of more than 6,000 Moorish troops, and together they headed deep into the Moroccan desert to wage war. On August 4, 1578, the armies clashed with Mulay Abdelmalek's Turkish forces outside the town of Alcácer Quibir. The battle, now known as the Battle of Three Kings, due to the trio of combined forces it involved, was short yet bloody, with both sides losing over 7,000 men. And in the melee, King Sebastian I vanished.

Although reports of what happened to Sebastian vary, he is said to have been last seen riding his horse fiercely into the fray but is presumed to have either been killed in the fighting or else captured, taken prisoner, and executed shortly afterward. Regardless of his fate, however, when news of the young king's untimely death broke back in Portugal, the country was thrown into disarray.

With no son and heir to take his place, Sebastian's throne fell to his great uncle, Henry — the 66-year-old brother of the former king, John III — who quickly found control over the grieving country difficult to maintain. Worsening the situation, Henry died barely two years after his unexpected ascent to the throne, and so in 1580, Portugal was thrown into a bitter succession crisis that eventually spiraled into an equally bitter conflict. The War of the Portuguese Succession, as it became known, went on to cripple the country for the next three years.

Against this backdrop, many Portuguese people struggled to come to terms with the death of young King Sebastian. Even when King Henry himself claimed to have received Sebastian's body from the Moroccan kingdom and given his remains a full royal burial in Lisbon, many people refused to believe that the body was his and that their adventurous leader had indeed perished on foreign soil. The succession crisis only served to worsen the people's grief and rumors soon began to emerge that Sebastian had fled the battlefield in Morocco, survived the war, or else had escaped captivity — and moreover that he would one day return home to Portugal to rule his flourishing kingdom once more.

Even as the decades went by and the country's succession crisis was resolved, the legend of Portugal's lost king endured. Countless imposters and pretenders to the throne claiming to be Sebastian came and went, and even as a new century dawned the belief that the King was still alive and would return to save Portugal persisted. The faith of Sebastian's supporters became so strong that a cult of "Sebastianism" was founded, and proved so influential that when a new king, John IV, was crowned in 1640, he was made to agree that he would surrender the throne should Sebastian I ever return to Portugal, even though, by that time, the "young" King Sebastian would have been well into his 80s.

By the early 18th century, now more than a hundred years after Sebastian's death, this bizarre cult of Sebastianism had become ever more mystical, with its followers eventually imagining that their (now long deceased) king would return as a Messiah, purely in a spiritual form, and would rise from the dead to return Portugal to its former glory. And despite the cult's increasingly impossible expectations, its numbers nevertheless continued to grow.

Eventually, however, common sense prevailed. By the 1800s, the cultish Sebastianism movement had largely disappeared. One of history's most peculiar episodes, it seemed, was finally over.

CHAPTER 37

JUST DESERTS

The Sonoran Desert in the far southwest corner of the United States regularly reaches temperatures over 105°F and sees barely half an inch of rainfall across the entire year. That might make it an unlikely place to find a lake, but remarkably, California's vast, shallow, and highly saline Salton Sea stands at the desert's northern end.

Sandwiched between the city of San Diego and Joshua Tree National Park; the sea, which is really a rift lake, formed in a depression along the southern tip of the San Andreas Fault, covers some 340 square miles. But even more remarkable than that, the desert not only has a sea, it allegedly has a shipwreck.

Legendary stories about a treasure-laden Spanish galleon lost somewhere beneath the sands of the Californian, Nevadan, or Arizonan desert have endured for centuries, with the first tales thought to have emerged sometime in the 18th century. The Gold Rushes and Land Rushes of the 1800s helped make these stories more widely known, so that by the tail end of the 19th century, the lost ships of the deserts of California were being immortalized in books, poems, and folk songs. Meanwhile, many luckless prospectors had even tried launching expeditions deep into the desert, in vain attempts to locate their treasures.

So is there any truth behind these tales? And is there any chance of an ancient ship being lost somewhere in the desert? Oddly, it could be argued that there is, and that these tales are not quite as bizarre as they might sound.

Back when Spanish colonists were first exploring and settling the west coast of North America in the 1600s, many of the region's inland seas and lakes were still connected to the coast by narrow streams and tributaries. Most of these ancient waterways have long since been dammed and had their waters redirected for agricultural or domestic use, or else have dried up entirely due to climate change or the changing landscape of the area. But according to some versions of the lost ship legend, a Spanish galleon laden with gold and pearls sailed inland from the Pacific Ocean along one of these rivers, propelled along by an unseasonable high tide in the Gulf of California. Some 100 miles inland, the ship was struck by a sudden deluge of floodwater coming the other way from the Colorado River and capsized. As the floods and the tidal waters receded, the ship became stranded on dry land and was eventually lost beneath the shifting desert sands.

Another version of the tale claims that a ship became stranded in the Salton Sea basin by a mudslide or a landslip triggered by thunderstorms, floodwaters, or even an earthquake. Yet another version claims that the ship became stranded in the basin when an unusually powerful tidal bore (i.e. a wall of water swept inland by a high tide) knocked clean through a giant levee or land barrier beside the Salton Sea and swept the ship into the basin. This latter tale might seem unlikely, but in 1922 an exceptionally strong 15ft tall bore swept along the Colorado River with such force that it indeed managed to capsize a steamboat, killing perhaps as many as 100 of its passengers.

As unlikely as these tales may seem at first glance, they are neither without precedence, nor are they impossible. But if a ship were to be lost somewhere in the deserts of the southwest United States, we can presume that it has long been swamped by sand and now resides somewhere hidden from view. Whether it will ever be seen or found again remains to be seen!

CHAPTER 38

ROYAL RUMBLE

Of all England's kings and queens, Henry VIII must certainly be one of the most well-known. The second of England's Tudor monarchs, Henry is perhaps best remembered for his string of turbulent marriages, that are now so well known that a famous rhyme immortalizing their fates, "divorced, beheaded, died; divorced, beheaded, survived", has slipped into popular culture.

Besides being history's most well-married king, Henry also set in motion the rift from the Catholic Church that led to the formation of the Anglican branch of Christianity and the so-called Dissolution of the Monasteries, which saw him launch devastating attacks on religious institutions all across his kingdom that refused to accept his newly created church. During his rule, he also secured an English victory over Scotland at the famous Battle of Flodden; warred with his unending string of cardinals and advisors, including Thomas More, Thomas Cromwell, and Cardinal Wolsey; and found the time to father no less than three future English monarchs, namely his children Edward VI, Mary I, and Elizabeth I.

But of all the events in Henry VIII's life, perhaps one of the least well known, and arguably one of the most unusual - took place during a lavish royal summit in northern France in 1520.

At that time, much of Western Europe was under the control of three young, powerful, and ambitious rulers: 29-year-old Henry VIII in England, 23-year-old Francis I of France, and 20-year-old Charles V of Spain. Two years earlier, in 1518, the three young kings—along with several other western rulers—had signed a treaty, agreeing to set aside any mutual hostilities and together they would fight against the growing threat of the Ottoman regime in eastern Europe. That treaty had united the three kings not only politically but personally, and so together the rulers were considered to be on good terms.

But in 1519, Charles V was suddenly elected ruler of the Holy Roman Empire, a disparate collection of states and territories incorporating much of central and southern Europe. As such, Charles now controlled an enormous amount of the continent, as well as his native Kingdom of Spain. This developed led to a sudden and uneasy imbalance between the three united kings, and so in response England and France started to seek a secondary alliance, combining their two forces in an attempt to equal those now wielded by King Charles.

It fell to Cardinal Wolsey to make arrangements for the alliance, and under his guidance, a grand conference was arranged at Balinghem, in northeastern France, at which the two sides could meet, negotiate terms, and celebrate their coalition. Both of the young kings, however, had something of a macho reputation to uphold, and as a result, both England and France viewed the conference as an opportunity to show off to the other side, and demonstrate their nation's flair, power, and culture.

What began merely as a political summit consequently soon morphed into a grand royal symposium, so vast and extravagant that it almost bankrupted both nations. Fountains of wine, enormous banquet halls, and even makeshift palaces were all erected to make the occasion more regal, while more than 3,000 sheep, 800 calves, and 300 oxen were brought on-site to keep the royal parties fed across the three-week event. The kings and their courts' negotiations were likewise housed in suitably luxurious accommodation, with a sea of gold-embroidered tents erected in a nearby meadow, stretching as far as the eye could see. It was from this spectacular sight that the ceremony eventually gained its suitably extravagant name: 'The Field of the Cloth of Gold'.

One of the centerpieces of the Field was a vast sports competition, at which the French and English kings' men could compete against one another in shows of fitness and military prowess. And, not wanting to be outdone, the two young kings were keen to join in with the games and festivities themselves. As a result, Henry VIII challenged the King of France to a wrestling match.

Both men were not only of similar age but were of similar athletic ability. Both were keen sportsmen and hunters too, and although Henry VIII went on to gain a reputation for his less-than-athletic frame in later life, in his twenties he was a strong, strapping young man. (He was also remarkably imposing: the average height of an English man in the Tudor period was 5' 4", whereas Henry stood an impressive 6' 1"!) It seems likely, then, that both kings must have fancied their chances against the other—but on this occasion, it was King Francis that came out victorious.

Precisely what happened in this royal rumble is unclear, but it seems Henry was initially keener to wrestle than Francis, who worried that a quick bout of hand-to-hand combat might sour their fledgling alliance. Nevertheless, Francis eventually agreed, and reportedly thanks to a clever French wrestling technique known as the "Breton Trip," promptly succeeded in throwing Henry VIII to the ground and claimed victory.

Happily, despite his infamously irascible temper, Henry seemingly took the defeat well and both kings walked away from the bout laughing and smiling. The English–French alliance was, for a short while at least, still intact.

CHAPTER 39

BY THE BYE

Throughout the country's long history, the United States' presidents have each achieved a remarkable set of honors, prizes, and firsts.

Woodrow Wilson is the only US president ever to have held a Ph.D. President Taft is the only person to have both held the presidency and served as 'Chief Justice of the Supreme Court'. On May 22, 1849, Abraham Lincoln became the first and only president to be granted a US patent, No. 6,469, for a device he designed that lifted boats over shoals. And in 2005, Bill Clinton became the first US president to win a Grammy Award, picking up the prize for Best Spoken Word Album for the audiobook of his autobiography, *My Life*. (Jimmy Carter went on to win the same award three times in 2007, 2016, and 2019, while Barrack Obama has won it twice before he became president, in 2006 and 2008.)

Of all the presidential achievements, however, one of the most bizarre is that of Thomas Jefferson, who, it could be argued, is responsible for inventing an entirely new way of saying "goodbye" that became a popular catchphrase across 19th-century America.

The story begins sometime around the start of Thomas Jefferson's second term as president, in the early 1800s. One day, he was out riding around his Monticello estate in Charlottesville, Virginia, when he happened to bump into a gentleman who was also out on his horse, and who accompanied him on the remainder of his trek. The man, it seems, failed to recognize that his new riding companion was the President of the United States, and the two men simply continued to chat casually as they rode along.

As it often does, however, the gentle small talk quickly turned to politics, and still blissfully unaware that he was riding with the President, the man began to angrily badmouth the entire current US administration, culminating in a vocal attack on President Jefferson himself. The Louisiana Purchase of 1803, the man declared, had been nothing but a "wild scheme." The 1807 Embargo Act - which halted trade in protest over the British and French treatment of America during the Napoleonic Wars - was a disastrous diplomatic misfire. And, according to this man, the president's plans for a so-called "gunboat navy" were even more preposterous. Throughout all the complaining and the angry invective, however, Jefferson remained resolutely silent.

Eventually, the pair arrived back at the road leading up to Jefferson's estate, and despite now knowing precisely what the man thought of him, the president calmly asked him if he would like to join him for a drink and some refreshment. The man gratefully accepted, and as he stepped down from his horse, finally decided the time was right to ask his new friend his name.

"Thomas Jefferson," the president replied. "And you?"

Suddenly, and at long, long last, the events of the previous hour or so dawned on the man, who paused for a moment before answering. "My name is Haines," he answered curtly, before jumping back up onto his horse and galloping away as fast as he could, without another word.

Jefferson, in typically self-effacing style, reportedly relished telling this particular tale to his friends and colleagues. The story had become well known enough to make its way into print for the first time in the early 1840s. Thanks to that, by the mid-19th century, "My name is Haines!" Had become a quirky and popular catchphrase in American slang. It was used whenever anyone needed to depart from somewhere quickly and without the usual formalities, or else whenever a terrible error was suddenly realized and the time had come to bail out of a conversation.

Sadly, the popularity of the phrase—like many catchphrases—proved short-lived, and its use in American English appears to have dwindled after the Civil War. By the turn of the century, few people, if any, were still using it. Nevertheless, Thomas Jefferson's peculiar contribution to our language remains recorded in one of the dustier corners of the dictionary to this day!

CHAPTER 40

CRAZY FACTS 5

1. Socrates used to dance around his house on his own to keep fit.

2. Around one in every 2,000 Japanese people is over 100 years old.

3. Allegedly, only two people in the world are permitted to know the recipe for Coca-Cola and company regulations demand that they never travel on the same airplane.

4. The English language had no word for the color orange until people in Europe began eating oranges in the 1500s. Before then, orange was called "red-yellow."

5. Jane Austen's funeral was attended by four people.

6. Because of the number of fireworks it uses, Disney World is the second-largest purchaser of explosives in the United States, after the US military.

7. It is impossible to breathe and swallow at the same time.

8. Elizabeth Taylor was late for her own funeral: She reportedly requested her coffin be brought into the church 15 minutes later than planned.

9. Mufasa's roar in *The Lion King* was the sound of a bear's roar, mixed with that of a tiger.

10. People have been wearing high-heeled shoes for more than 2000 years.

11. Hippopotamus skin is so thick that hippos are considered bulletproof.

12. As well as humans, gorillas, and chimpanzees also have fingerprints. But koala fingerprints are so similar to human fingerprints that even forensic scientists have found it difficult to tell the two apart.

13. *Psycho* was the first American movie to show a flushing toilet.

14. Frank Welker, who provided the voice for Fred in the *Scooby Doo* animated series, also recorded the sounds made by the monkeys in *Jumanji* and *Aladdin*, plus recorded Spock's scream in *Star Trek III: The Search for Spock.*

15. President Jimmy Carter once sent a jacket to his dry cleaner with the United States nuclear detonation codes still in his pocket.

CHAPTER 41

AN OCTOPUS' ARMORS

For centuries, natural scientists understood the use of tools as an aid in certain day-to-day tasks to be an exclusive feature of human beings—a defining sign of our superior intelligence, compared to the lesser creatures of the animal kingdom.

More recently, however, that viewpoint has been forced to change, as more and more creatures have been observed using makeshift equipment in the natural world.

Among the most famous of nature's tool-users are primates. Chimpanzees, human beings' closest animal relatives, have long been observed using projectiles to hunt prey, and use pointed sticks and similar tools to catch ants and feed off honey. Chimps have been busying themselves in nature's toolbox for many thousands of years: Archeological researchers studying an ancient chimpanzee habitat in the Côte d'Ivoire, on the west coast of Africa, have found evidence of the use of stone striking tools among chimp communities dating back more than 4,000 years.

Gorillas too have been found to use sticks to aid in walking and foraging, use boughs from trees and shrubs to cross flooded land, and have even been witnessed using poles to test the depth of murky water. While Sumatran orangutans have been observed using stones to smash open tough nuts and seeds, and use long sticks to "fish" fruit from out-of-reach branches.

It's not just primates that share our love of makeshift gadgets and gizmos. Sea otters famously break open shellfish on flat stone paddles held on their chests. Lammergeyer vultures carry bones high into the sky and drop them onto boulders to smash them into easier to swallow shards. Elephants have been seen to use branches as flyswatters (and according to anecdotal evidence at least, to use rocks and heavy tree trunks to short out the power boxes on electrified fences). And perhaps most remarkable of all, a captive cockatoo has recently been observed shaping and using peeled strips of wood to retrieve otherwise unreachable objects, on the outside of its cage.

Far from being exclusive to humans, then, tool use seems quite widespread in the animal kingdom, and has even been observed below the waves.

One of the latest animals added to the ever-lengthening list of creatures that use tools is the octopus. What makes this case even more remarkable, however, is that the octopus in question uses its tools not to find or retrieve food but to camouflage and protect itself.

The veined octopus is a species found in the tropical seas of the western Pacific Ocean, where it preys on shellfish, including shrimp, crabs, and clams, in warm, sandy-bottomed bays and lagoons. The species first came to scientific attention in 2005, when an octopus off the coast of Indonesia was found to have adopted an almost unique method of moving around the seafloor: pulling six of its tentacles in against its body, the veined octopus uses its two remaining tentacles to "walk" bipedally across the seabed. Quite why the veined octopus "walks" in this manner is unclear, but it has been suggested that it may be an attempt at camouflage, by pulling its remaining legs into its body, the octopus may be trying to mimic the coconuts that so often bob through the shallow waters it inhabits.

More recently, however, in 2009, another veined octopus made headlines when researchers at the University of Melbourne observed it using debris from the seafloor in an ingenious and unique way. The octopus was found to collect discarded half coconut shells from the sea bed and, using its sucker-covered tentacles, arrange the shells around its body to form a makeshift armor. This tough plating ultimately provides the octopus with some much-needed rigid protection for its otherwise soft and fairly vulnerable body. This is believed to be the first known example of a sea creature producing defensive covering for itself.

CHAPTER 42

FOR THE BIRDS

Whether it is horses ridden fearlessly into battle, or the ancient general Hannibal crossing the Alps with his troops of "war elephants," for almost as long as human beings have engaged in war, we have enlisted help from animals to do so. And in the conflicts of the first half of the 20th century, one of the most important animals we conscripted into our forces was also one of the humblest and most unlikely.

During World War I and II, many thousands of homing pigeons were used to ferry written messages from the front line back to command headquarters; the American forces utilized more than 600 pigeons in their French campaign alone. The birds could fly swiftly and accurately, and at such an altitude to make shooting them from the sky all but impossible. What's more, unlike radio and telegraph messages, the pigeons' messages could not be scrambled, nor interfered with, required no electrical supply to be communicated, and took up less space than heavy and bulky transmission equipment. Many World War I tanks had room inside to keep a brood of pigeons so that messages could be relayed from the front line even within the most brutal battles.

It was during one of these World War I efforts that one pigeon made an almost unbelievable contribution to the Allies' campaign.

The Meuse-Argonne Offensive was one of the longest, bloodiest, and fortunately latest episodes of the Great War. Lasting almost four weeks, the campaign took place in northern France in late September of 1918 and involved more than one million Allied soldiers — over 25,000 of those, would lose their lives. And in the midst of all of this, a so-called "Lost Battalion" of 500 men became stranded at the foot of a hillside valley, surrounded by German troops. After just one day of fighting from this unenviable situation, barely 200 of the men remained alive.

To make matters worse, the Allied forces had no clue that this stranded battalion was there and, presuming the area to be fully swamped with German troops, began shelling the entire hillside. If the men were not able to get word back to their side, they would be killed by Allied friendly fire long before the German troops surrounding them even managed to advance.

The commander of the stranded men, Major Charles Whittlesey, knew that his and his men's only chance of survival lay with the trio of carrier pigeons they had with them. Messages were written, but the first two birds the men released were shot down almost instantly by the surrounding German forces. The men's survival, ultimately, rested with their final pigeon — known as "Cher Ami", which was released with a simple message reading: "We are along the road parallel to 276.4. Our own artillery is dropping a barrage directly on us. For heaven's sake, stop it."

Against all odds, Cher Ami escaped the rain of gunfire that commenced almost the moment he was sent up into the air and flew the 25 miles back to the Allied lines. He landed, having been shot in the breast and blinded in one eye, with the lost men's message dangling perilously from a bloodied, almost severed leg. The Allies, however, managed to read the note, ceased their shelling instantly, and were eventually able to organize a military advancement on the enemy territory to break the battalion out and return them to safety. Cher Ami's extraordinary journey, against all odds and while suffering some truly terrible injuries, had saved the lives of some 200 men.

Incredibly, Cher Ami survived his ordeal but never fully recovered from his injuries and died the following year back at Fort Monmouth, in New Jersey. His body was saved, taxidermied, and is today on display in the Smithsonian Museum.

Before his death, however, Cher Ami's remarkable tale was recognized in an equally remarkable way: he was awarded the *Croix de Guerre (1914–1918)*, a French military medal usually only handed out to French and Allied soldiers who had performed especially valorous service during World War I. As a Croix de Guerre honoree, ultimately, Cher Ami took his place alongside the likes of Charles de Gaulle, US Generals George S Patton and Douglas MacArthur, and British fighter-ace pilot Vernon Castle.

CHAPTER 43

STARS WARRED

Few movies have attracted as great a following and fandom as 1977's *Star Wars*, the first movie in what has become a nine-part series and a multi-billion dollar franchise. The original 1977 movie alone earned more than $750 million at the box office and went on to be nominated for ten Academy Awards—including Best Picture and Best Director. Sound designer Ben Burtt received a special citation Oscar award for his achievements in creating the bizarre mixture of noises for the movie's cast of alien creatures and robots.

Another of *Star Wars'* Academy Award nominees was the acclaimed English actor Sir Alec Guinness, whose performance as Jedi Master Obi-Wan Kenobi brought some much-needed respectability and dramatic gravitas to the movie. Despite it securing him his 5th Oscar nomination, however—and despite the enduring success and popularity of the movie—Guinness himself was not too enamored with *Star Wars*. Over the years, clues as to just how little he enjoyed the movie and its production have continued to come to light.

"I have returned to London this evening for my stint at the studio for the rest of the week," Guinness wrote to his friend

Anne Kaufman during a break in filming in 1976, before adding, "Can't say I'm enjoying the film. New rubbish dialogue reaches me every other day on wads of pink paper — and none of it makes my character clear or even bearable. I just think, thankfully, of the lovely bread [i.e. money] which will help me keep going."

The following day, Guinness wrote once more to Kaufman, giving some tantalizing details of just how bizarre a movie *Star Wars* was to work on. "I must head off to studio and work with a dwarf," he wrote — adding that the actor in question, Kenny Baker (who portrayed the droid R2-D2), was, "very sweet — and he has to wash in a bidet!"

Guinness may not have been able to recall Kenny Baker's name, but it seems he had just as much trouble with the film's now legendary leads too. When it came to listing his co-stars, Guinness correctly remembered the name of, "Your fellow countryman Mark Hamill," who played Luke Skywalker, but struggled when it came to remembering who had been cast as Han Solo. "Tennyson (that can't be right) Ford," he wrote, before guessing again, then finally giving up. "Ellison (? — No!) — well, a rangy, languid young man who is probably intelligent and amusing. But Oh, God, God, they make me feel ninety — and treat me as if I was 106." Happily, Guinness did eventually remember his co-star's name, by adding a footnote to his letter: "*Harrison Ford*," he wrote at the bottom of the page. "Ever heard of him?"

He may not have quite known what he let himself in for when he took on the role of Obi-Wan, but Alec Guinness at least took his Oscar nomination from the *Star Wars* filming process.

Once a sequel was mooted, however, Guinness was not keen to reprise his role and reportedly wanted absolutely nothing to do with the next film in the series, *The Empire Strikes Back*.

Director George Lucas, knowing that Guinness' role was still imperative to the story, eventually convinced Guinness to appear in the follow-up movie, albeit almost entirely on his terms: his single scene had to be shot in one day between the hours of 8 a.m. and 1 p.m. and in lieu of a fee he was paid a quarter of 1% of the film's full box office gross. With that deal set in stone, Guinness' five hours of work on *The Empire Strikes Back* eventually earned him more than $450,000.

What he thought of the film itself, however, we don't know.

CHAPTER 44

WHICH WITCH

Looking back through history, it's often surprising to find that many things happen somewhat later or earlier than we might expect. The last time the guillotine was used in a French execution, for instance, was 1977—the same year that Apple was founded, *Star Wars* was released at the cinemas, and Stephen King published *The Shining*. The first time someone wrote the letters "OMG," on the other hand, was not in a text message in the early 2000s, but in a letter to Winston Churchill in 1917.

Another equally anachronistic event took place in the UK in 1944—when the British legal system imprisoned the last person in its history to be tried as a witch.

The woman in question was Helen Duncan, a 47-year-old housewife from the town of Callendar in Perthshire, Scotland. The mother of six children, to make ends meet, Duncan held down part-time jobs in a local infirmary and a bleach-producing factory. Her main calling, however, was as a medium and paranormalist; a skill which would eventually bring her considerable fame and success. (In fact, if legend is to be believed, even the likes of Winston Churchill and the future King George VI called on Duncan's services during her lifetime.)

Duncan's involvement with the paranormal allegedly began in childhood, when she gained a reputation at her school for terrifying her classmates (and, for that matter, her devout Presbyterian mother) with various spiritual prognostications and rambling prophecies of doom. In her 20's, now encouraged by her husband and young family, she turned to mediumship as a means of expounding her interest in the supernatural. She began holding séances in her home in Scotland. As her notoriety grew, Duncan began to be invited to hold séances all across the United Kingdom and became known not only for being able to summon and communicate with the spirits of the dead but also supposedly to produce a pale, slimy ectoplasm from her mouth as she did so.

Duncan's skills, such as they were, soon became well known enough that in 1928 a photographer was called on to document her talents. But to many people's obvious disappointment, the photographs he produced, which reportedly showed Duncan summoning a spirit, as well as calling upon her ghostly spirit guide "Peggy", were quite clearly staged. Peggy and her fellow spirits were comprised of nothing more than faces cut out of magazines and poorly made papier-mâché masks atop thick white cotton sheets.

Soon afterward, a series of experiments were arranged, but these too proved that Duncan was perhaps not quite as spiritually connected as she claimed to be. The ectoplasm she was said to produce from her mouth was found to be nothing more than a mixture of egg white and various other kitchen

137

staples. Duncan's angry refusal to be X-rayed—during an attempt to prove that there was no medical explanation for her abilities; led one investigator to rightly deduce that Duncan kept this slime in cheesecloth pouches in her mouth and gullet. While claiming to be speaking to the dead, Duncan would regurgitate the pouches and burst them open to produce a stream of gunge from her mouth.

Finally, her apparent fakery proved too much, and when Duncan claimed to have summoned the spirit of a young girl, seen emerging out of the darkness behind her at a séance in Edinburgh, one of the attendees quickly became suspicious. They turned on the lights and grabbed the spirit, only to find that it was a not particularly well-made knitted doll! As a result of that particular stunt, Duncan was convicted of fraudulent mediumship at the Edinburgh Sheriff Court in 1933, and fined £10.

Despite her credentials seemingly not holding up to much scrutiny, Duncan was still able to continue her career as a medium. By the end of the decade, she was still very much in demand. But at a séance in the city of Portsmouth in 1941, she finally overstepped the mark once and for all.

By that time, World War II had been rumbling on for two years. The parents of a young man who had enlisted with the Royal Navy, but had never been heard from again, contacted Duncan to ask if she could shed some light on their son's fate, as well as that of his ship, the HMS *Barham*. Professing to have spoken to her spirit guides, Duncan confirmed that the young man's ship had indeed been sunk and that he, along with all of his fellow crewmates, had perished.

This time, at least, Duncan's story was entirely true: The *Barham* had indeed been sunk just a few weeks earlier, by a German U-boat off the Mediterranean coast of Egypt, with the loss of all those on board. At that time, however, the sinking had been concealed by the Royal Navy's Board of Admiralty in an attempt to bolster British morale and avoid Germany claiming the sinking as a propagandizing victory. Duncan's apparent knowledge of the sinking, at a time when its occurrence was still highly censored, brought her to the attention of the authorities, and as the war continued, Duncan remained under scrutiny.

Eventually, the events of the war began to come to their bloody conclusion and Britain began to make arrangements for the D-Day landings, again, with intense secrecy. As a result, any potential leaking of military maneuvers was taken very seriously, and with Duncan still viewed with suspicion by the military authorities, two Royal Navy lieutenants were dispatched to attend one of her séances in January 1944. The two men were horrified by what they found: Duncan claimed to be in contact with the spirit of one attendee's dead sister (despite his sister being alive and well and living in London), while a spirit that emerged from behind a curtain during the séance was eventually revealed to be Duncan herself dressed in a fairly unconvincing white sheet. The police were called, and Duncan soon found herself in court charged with "public mischief," obtaining money by false pretenses, and in a crime that would land her a place in the history books, in contravention of Section 4 of the 1735 Witchcraft Act, which outlawed "fraudulent spiritual activity." For her crimes, Duncan was sentenced to nine months in prison.

On her release from jail in 1945, Duncan swore to stop conducting séances, but was later arrested holding another one a decade later in 1956. She died later that same year, at the age of 59.

CHAPTER 45

MUSIC ROYALTY

Queen Elizabeth II is known for owning several corgi dogs, a striking collection of hats and handbags, the Crown Jewels, no fewer than six royal residences and, of course, the best seat in the Royal Box at the Wimbledon Tennis Club.

As well as all of that, however, the Queen technically owns almost half of the entire coastline of the United Kingdom (thanks to the official leases of her "Crown Estate" portfolio of land). She also famously can claim ownership of all the swans on the River Thames, due to an ancient 15th-century agreement overseen by two equally ancient English organizations called the Worshipful Company of Vintners and the Worshipful Company of Dyers. Plus, thanks to an even older law dating back to 1235, which, incredibly, remains on Britain's statute books to this day, the Queen can also lay claim to all of the whales, sturgeon fish, dolphins, and porpoises in the UK's waters, up to three miles out from the British shore. (Until recently, the Queen also technically owned all of the shellfish caught in Scotland's waters as part of her Crown Estate, but that law has since been repealed. She does, however, lay claim to all of Scotland's gold mines!)

Also among the Queen's more unusual possessions, however, is an official gold record, presented to her by the Official Charts Company, which is charge of recording music sales in the United Kingdom. It's a prize typically only awarded to rock stars and best-selling pop singers, so how has the Queen come to be the recipient of one?

If you're thinking that you'd like to hear what the Queen's singing voice sounds like, then unfortunately you are going to be disappointed. No, the gold record is not actually in recognition of a vocal recording made by the Queen herself. Instead, it recognizes a remarkable record set by a recording the Queen merely oversaw as part of her golden jubilee celebrations in 2002.

On June 4, 2002, to celebrate Queen Elizabeth II's impressive 50 years on the British throne, a grand star-studded outdoor concert was arranged to take place at the Queen's official London residence, Buckingham Palace. Among the parade of legendary performers on the playbill were the likes of Paul McCartney, Tony Bennett, Elton John, Shirley Bassey, Brian Wilson, Bryan Adams, Eric Clapton, Phil Collins, Tom Jones, and Annie Lennox. Even Ozzy Osbourne took part in the show; ironically enough, so too did both the legendary British rock band Queen and the cast of the Queen musical, *We Will Rock You*.

Given its A-list attendees, the concert proved hugely successful, and several weeks later a recording of the performance was released by record label EMI. The recording sold an incredible 100,000 copies in the first week of its release alone, and in recognition of the achievement, the Official

Charts Company sent Her Majesty a gold disc; despite her vocals, alas, not appearing on the recording at all.

To this day, the Queen remains the only member of the royal family ever to be awarded a gold record in recognition of album sales.

CHAPTER 46

HORROR MOVIE

John Wayne is one of Hollywood's most legendary performers, the Oscar-winning star of such movies as *True Grit*, *Stagecoach*, *The Searchers*, and *The Quiet Man*. In a career full of movie gold, however, it's no surprise that Wayne has also made a few box office turkeys along the way too—most notable of all, arguably, 1956's *The Conqueror*.

Directed by Dick Powell, *The Conqueror* was a historical retelling of the life of the brutal 13th-century Mongol warlord Genghis Khan. Wayne, of course, played the eponymous conqueror, but never one of the most versatile actors, his performance is now considered one of Hollywood's greatest miscastings. At the box office, the movie initially made back barely two-thirds of its enormous $6 million budget. Today, it's widely considered one of the weakest movies of the Golden Age of Hollywood, and one of the biggest duds in John Wayne's long and otherwise impressive career.

There is, however, a more sinister reason why *The Conqueror* remains talked about today.

The movie was filmed at various locations across the state of

Utah, among them Leeds, Snow Canyon, and Harrisburg. But many of its grand exterior shots were filmed in and around St. George, a remote city in Washington County — which, at the time, stood barely 130 miles downwind of the United States government's Nevada National Security Site. It was there in the heat of the desert sun, and at the tail end of World War Two, that the government and Manhattan Project scientists had conducted a series of devastating nuclear weapon tests a decade earlier. And the region around St. George, though declared safe at the time, received the brunt of nuclear fallout from this long period of testing.

The government reportedly chose the location so that the prevailing wind in the area would carry the fallout from the blasts away from the more heavily populated areas of Vegas and Los Angeles to the southwest and instead toward what was classed as the "virtually uninhabitable" land downwind. The production team behind *The Conqueror*, meanwhile, chose the area, believing it to be safe, because its vast "uninhabitable" landscape resembled the open wastelands of Genghis Khan's Mongolian Empire.

Concerns were raised during filming about the safety of the area; an infamous photograph even shows John Wayne operating a Geiger counter on set, which reportedly crackled so loudly when he turned it on that he initially thought it was broken. Their worries were short-lived and shrugged off, however, as reassurances came from the Federal Government that the area was indeed safe to film in. As a result, the cast and crew spent several grueling weeks filming battle scenes in and around St. George and Snow Canyon, blissfully unaware of just how toxic the landscape truly was.

A later investigation proved that, of the 220 cast and crew who were involved in the shoot, more than 90 developed medical conditions related to exposure to radiation—including Wayne himself and his co-stars Susan Hayward, Agnes Moorehead, and Pedro Armendáriz, all of whom succumbed to cancers eventually tied to their time on set in Utah in the 1970s. The director Dick Powell, too, died of cancer just seven years after the film was released.

Meanwhile, the producer Howard Hughes—though unaffected by the shoot himself, reportedly felt so guilty for arranging the filming locations (despite the government advice telling him it was safe) that he spent more than $10 million purchasing every print of the movie, and effectively removed all trace of it from circulation. The film remained out of circulation until after Hughes' death in 1976, when his library of movies was purchased by Universal Studios. As well as not being critically well-received, the aftermath of *The Conqueror* has ultimately become one of Hollywood's darkest and bitterest scandals.

CHAPTER 47

A GRAND TOUR

Everyone does foolish things when they've had one too many drinks.

In 2015, French police reported discovering a 22-year-old intoxicated man in a shipyard in Brittany in northern France, attempting to give lifesaving CPR to an inflatable dinghy, believing it to be a dying person. In 2017, newspapers in New Zealand reported that a man had woken up to find his car had been stolen and called the police—who promptly discovered that the man had sold the car to a friend the previous evening when he ran out of cash. And in 2018, an Estonian holidaymaker in the Italian Alps took a wrong turn while walking back to his hotel and ended up climbing up the side of a 2,400ft mountain after a little bit too much *après ski*. Even the occasional celebrity can fall foul of the demon drink, too: while living in Dublin in the 1960s, the legendary actor Peter O'Toole once bought a pub when the landlord refused to serve him another drink. Thankfully, a few hasty telephone calls to his accountant the following day—as well as a groveling meeting with the pub's landlord, who went on to become one of O'Toole's dearest friends—stopped him from bankrupting himself!

Few people have the means to purchase a bar outright, of course, but that's not to say that they can't make rash financial decisions when they're under the influence. But likewise, few people end up doing something daft when they're drunk that ends up costing them more than $2,000...

In the early hours of January 1, 2018, a Norwegian man (who, perhaps for obvious reasons, has declined ever to be named) stumbled drunkenly into a taxi in the Danish capital of Copenhagen after a few too many drinks seeing in the New Year. As is usual, the man told the driver his destination and the car set off into the night, while the man, suffering the after effects of his big night on the town, fell asleep in the back seat.

Nothing too outlandish yet, you might think? That's true, except for the fact that the man's destination was the Norwegian city of Oslo, more than 370 miles away.

The driver, it seems, happily set off on the unusually lengthy trip, first crossing the enormous Øresund Bridge from Denmark to Sweden, to arrive in the Swedish city of Malmo. From there, he headed north along the Swedish coast, passing the cities of Helsingborg and Gothenburg, eventually crossing the border into neighboring Norway, and arriving in Oslo some six and a half hours — and a whole three countries — later. It was at that point that the driver finally told his passenger the cost of his journey: 18,000 Norwegian kroner — equivalent to more than $2,200.

Unfortunately, when confronted with his somewhat unexpected bill, the man became belligerent, refused to pay the fee, and instead staggered into his home, locked the door, and promptly fell asleep. The furious taxi driver, for his part, was unable to wake him up to settle. Worse, on returning to his car, he found that his battery had died. With little else to do, he called the police.

The following morning, the man—who, Norwegian police noted, had no previous criminal record—sobered up and came to his senses, and thankfully agreed to pay the bill. Meanwhile, a recovery vehicle was called for the taxi driver, who was ultimately able to make his return to Denmark (albeit after a somewhat longer shift than normal...)

CHAPTER 48

CRAZY FACTS 6

1. The saxophone is called so because it was invented by a Belgian man named Adolphe Sax.

2. A Swedish woman who lost her wedding ring in her garden in 1995 found it 17 years later — around a carrot that had grown through it.

3. Woodpeckers' tongues are so long that they wrap around the backs of their skulls.

4. The coat of arms of the Russian town of Zheleznogorsk depicts a golden bear fighting with the nucleus of a plutonium atom. The town was founded in 1950 for the production of weapons-grade nuclear material.

5. The official bird of Redondo Beach, California, is the Goodyear Blimp.

6. A rainbow that happens at night is called a moon-bow.

7. Russia has a larger surface area than Pluto.

8. The funeral of William the Conqueror in 1087 was interrupted by a heckler, who shouted from the back of the church that it had been built on his father's land

without his family being compensated.

9. Queen Elizabeth II is fluent in French.

10. The deep-sea barreleye fish has a transparent dome for a head.

11. Some hummingbirds' hearts beat more than 1,200 times per minute.

12. In 2006, a man from Brisbane, Australia, tried to sell New Zealand on eBay, listing it as a country with "very ordinary weather." The sale price had reached more than $3,000 before eBay pulled the listing from their site.

13. Russia arrived 12 days late to the 1908 Olympics because they were still using the Julian calendar.

14. Dean Martin once worked as a croupier in an illegal speakeasy.

15. Agatha Christie gave her grandson the rights to her 1952 play *The Mousetrap* for his 7th birthday. The rights included a stipulation that the play never be adapted for the cinema until at least six months after the play stopped being performed in London's West End. The play is now the longest-running production in theatre history — and, as a result, it has still never been filmed.

CHAPTER 49

JUMPING INTO
THE HISTORY BOOKS

One of the problems with inventing something is that the time eventually arrives when you have to test your invention out, which usually involves testing it yourself. That's not so bad when it comes to testing something relatively harmless. Galileo, for instance, used his newly refined telescope design to discover the moons of Jupiter in 1610, while the inventor of the camera, Joseph Nicéphore Niépce, tested his invention out by simply snapping a picture of his Burgundy country estate in 1827. But if you've invented something potentially more dangerous, then the task is a little different.

In 1903, for instance, a General Electric employee named William Nelson was killed when he crashed a prototype motorized bicycle he had invented. In 1921, a Soviet inventor named Valerian Abakovsky died when a high-speed, airplane-powered railcar he had designed called the Aerowagon derailed on the railway tracks between Moscow and the city of Tula. Additionally, in 1928, a Russian physician named Alexander Bogdanov died when he gave himself a blood transfusion infected with malaria and tuberculosis as part of an ill-fated quest to achieve human rejuvenation.

Another person who tragically succumbed to a creation of their own was an Austrian-born French inventor named Franz Reichelt. What made Reichelt's invention so remarkable, however, was that he decided to test his design very publicly, before a crowd of spectators, at one of the world's most famous landmarks.

Reichelt was a tailor by trade, working in Paris in the early 20th century, when aviation was a burgeoning field. He became interested in potentially using his skills cutting fabric and tailoring garments to create a portable working parachute. As luck would have it, in 1911 a Colonel Lalance of the aeronautical "Aéro-Club de France" instituted a cash prize of 10,000 francs to anyone who could create a parachute, suitable for the club's aviators, that did not exceed 25kg (55lbs) in weight. Spurred on by the prize, Reichelt threw himself into his design work. Ultimately, he came up with what he called a "coat parachute," or "parachute suit" — a wearable, cape-like outfit that (should the need ever arise) could billow out behind its wearer and lower them safely to the ground.

After several months' work refining his design, in late 1911 Reichelt announced to the Paris press that he had obtained permission from the city authorities to test his design on a mannequin, which he would dress in his parachute and throw from the top of the Eiffel Tower. A date was arranged, and at 8:00 a.m. on February 4, 1912, Reichelt, along with a few supporters, a photographer, and a journalist, climbed the stairs of the Eiffel Tower, hauling his prototype parachute with him.

On the ground, 187ft beneath him, a large crowd of spectators and as many as 30 more journalists had gathered to watch, eager to witness yet another step forward in the history of aviation. Perhaps encouraged by attracting such a large crowd — and perhaps keen to take his place in the history books, at the last minute, Reichelt foolishly decided that rather than throw a mannequin from the Tower, he would take the opportunity to test his parachute himself. The friends and supporters who were with him tried to persuade him not to, but Reichelt was adamant. "I want to try the experiment myself and without trickery," he explained, "as I intend to prove the worth of my invention."

At 8:22 a.m., Reichelt stepped out onto the guard rail of the Tower, paused to test the speed and direction of the wind by dropping a loose slip of paper into the air, and, after a final pause, jumped from the Eiffel Tower. It was an immensely brave stunt. It was also his last.

Almost immediately after jumping, Reichelt became tangled in the loose fabric of his parachute. The 300 square feet of silk that should have billowed out behind him, to create a 16ft tall dome, decelerating his fall, failed to do so. Swamped by the folds of cloth, Reichelt hurtled to the ground below. He died instantly, becoming yet another brave yet tragic entry in the often uncompromising history of invention.

CHAPTER 50

TAKING THE PEE

Throughout history, rulers and despots all over the world have sought to impose levies on all kinds of unlikely things.

Hearths, windows, candles, and even soap have all been taxed at some time or another in England, as have playing cards, the ornate design of the ace of spades developing from the official insignias of printing houses, used to prove that the requisite duties had been paid. For centuries before the French revolution, salt was taxed in France. One of the oldest taxes we know of was a tax on cooking oil imposed by the pharaohs of Ancient Egypt more than 5,000 years ago. And in 1698, in a vain attempt to modernize his country, the Russian leader Peter the Great famously imposed a tax on any man wanting to sport a beard; the tax remained in place for the next 74 years.

But of all of history's most unusual taxes, perhaps the strangest—and easily the most unpleasant, was that imposed by the Roman emperor Vespasian in 70 CE.

As bizarre as it sounds, in Ancient Rome, human urine was a major commodity. The ammonia that could be extracted from it was used to bleach and clean the pristine white togas worn by Roman statesmen and noblemen, while urine could also be used in the production of wool and the tanning of leather, skins, and animal hides.

A tax on the collection and disposal of urine was first imposed on Rome in the 1st century CE, under Emperor Nero. Those who wished to purchase the urine collected in Rome's communal latrines were ultimately required to pay a tax on the quantity they bought. But Nero's original urine tax quickly proved unpopular and difficult to keep track of, and so was promptly repealed. When he died in 68 CE, the brief period of turmoil that followed, known as "The Year of the Four Emperors", quickly strained the city's coffers, so that when Vespasian finally took to the Roman throne in December 69 CE, the Roman state was perilously close to bankruptcy. Consequently, Vespasian felt compelled to reintroduce his predecessor's bizarre and unpopular tax, and Nero's urine-collecting levy was doled out once more on the people (and toilets) of Rome.

Happily, the tax later went on to be repealed for a second time, but not before it had two left two somewhat bizarre and lasting impacts on our language.

French urinals still to this day are known as *vespasiennes* in Emperor Vespasian's honor, the name being chosen as a euphemism in the early 1800s when a network of public restrooms was first opened across Paris. Meanwhile, according to the Roman historian Suetonius, when Vespasian's son Titus first heard about his father's urine tax, he expressed disgust that his father was trading and dealing in the purchase of urine. In response, Vespasian is said to have held up a gold coin in front of Titus' face and asked him if he thought it smelled. When Titus replied that it did not, Vespasian responded, "ah, and yet it comes from urine!" Suetonius' bizarre anecdote went on to inspire a famous Latin motto, *pecunia non olet!* - literally, "money does not stink!", which remains in use today as a reminder that it doesn't matter how you make money because it all has the same value.

CHAPTER 51

A RABBIT'S TALE

In September 1726, news of a story so remarkable that it was told to King George I himself, reached London: A 25-year-old woman named Mary Toft, in the village of Godalming in Surrey, had given birth to a litter of live rabbits. What followed this bizarre announcement was one of the most peculiar stories; and, as it was eventually revealed, hoaxes, in medical history.

According to the tale, earlier in 1726, Toft became pregnant yet tragically later lost her child. During her recovery and for several weeks afterward, however, Toft claimed that she had begun giving birth to mismatched animal parts, described by one physician at the time as resembling a "liverless cat," but reported by Toft and others elsewhere as a mixture of live and seemingly butchered rabbits.

"A poor woman who lives at Godalming," wrote one contemporary newspaper, "about a month past delivered ... a creature resembling a rabbit, but whose heart and lungs grew without its belly." The report continued that, "about 14 days since, she was delivered by the same ... a perfect Rabbit; and in a few days after of 4 more; and on Friday, Saturday,

Sunday, the 4th, 5th, and 6th instant, of one in each day: in all nine."

Amid reports that Toft remained quite visibly still pregnant seeming despite giving birth to nine rabbits, a local surgeon named John Howard was called. He reported that Toft was still producing animal limbs and organs. Bamboozled by the case, Howard sent reports of it to several of his fellow physicians and eventually brought the case to the attention of Nathaniel St André, the official surgeon to the royal household of King George I.

By now, Toft's bizarre case was the talk of London, and the royal family was intrigued enough to dispatch St André, along with Samuel Molyneux, the secretary to the Prince of Wales, to Godalming to investigate Toft in person. By the time the duo arrived in Surrey it was mid-November, yet St André wrote back to the King to say that Toft was indeed still producing rabbits and rabbit body parts. He elaborated further that, on investigation, they did indeed appear to be developing inside her body. Eventually, the case proved just too bizarre to ignore and arrangements were made for Toft to be brought down to London.

By late November, Toft had been presented to all of London's topmost physicians, who had each examined her and drawn conclusions of their own about her increasingly curious case. Some thought it a true marvel, an unsolvable mystery of nature; others were more suspicious, noting that the rabbits and rabbit parts Toft claimed to be producing appeared to come from near fully developed animals, appeared professional butchered and sliced up, and on further scrutiny, appeared to contain digested grass and other plant matter in their stomachs. As a result, those who were more doubtful of the case soon began to conduct enquiries into not only Toft herself but also of her house, her background, and, crucially her hometown, all in an attempt to unravel the mystery.

One such skeptical gentleman was Thomas Onslow, who traveled to Godalming and began asking around the local area for more context to Toft's case. There, Onslow heard news that Toft's husband Joshua had for several weeks now been purchasing young rabbits from a local butcher. This discovery fueled Onslow's suspicion, and he wrote back to London that he had uncovered evidence of what he believed to be a hoax, and would publish his findings as soon as possible.

Meanwhile, another of Toft's more suspicious physicians back in London recommended that she be put through a grueling surgical procedure to discover the true source of her bizarre case. It seems likely, however, that the physician was merely calling Toft's bluff; as soon as she was faced with the prospect of painful and intrusive surgery, and with Onslow's new evidence coming in from back home in Godalming, Toft finally confessed. The rabbits and rabbit parts had, she explained, been indeed supplied through a local butcher, and smuggled into her bedroom by her husband. The entire debacle, from the start, had been a hoax.

In the aftermath, Toft was arrested and imprisoned for the crime of "imposture," but was eventually released without charge. The physician who had initially publicized her case, meanwhile, was charged £800. There is no record of what happened to Toft after the case was revealed to be untrue, but no matter—by then, her place in medical history was assured.

CHAPTER 52

THE DRINKING AGE

The German composer Johann Sebastian Bach famously loved coffee so much that he wrote an entire ten-movement cantata about it. The so-called *Coffee Cantata,* or rather, as it is properly known, *Schweigt stille, plaudert nicht* ("Be still, stop chattering"); received its debut performance in a Leipzig coffeehouse in 1735. Throughout history, however, not everyone has shared Bach's enthusiasm.

In 1511, for instance, the governor of Mecca outlawed coffee because he believed that its stimulating effect promoted radical thinking. Likewise, when Murad IV ascended to the throne as Sultan of the Ottoman Empire in 1623, he instantly outlawed coffee on pain of a beating for a first offense and being thrown into the Bosporus Straits for a second offense. And when coffee first arrived in Italy, many of the country's most pious religious leaders labeled it a "satanic" influence and campaigned for it to be banned; it took Pope Clement VIII just one sip of the drink to turn down their request. He instead branded coffee so delicious a drink that it should be baptized!

Of all the historical figures who have tried to do away with everyone's cup of Joe; however, perhaps the most unwise was the Prussian leader King Frederick II.

Frederick ascended to the Prussian throne as King Frederick II in 1740 and ruled over the kingdom for the next 46 years, longer than any other of Prussia's legendary Hohenzollern dynasty of rulers. During his reign, Frederick greatly expanded Prussia's territory, its military, and its power and influence across Europe, as well as establishing a great many cultural institutions, forging a reputation as a tireless patron of the arts, and ensuring Prussian artists made a lasting impact on the European Enlightenment. For all of that, he rightly became known to his people as Frederick the Great.

One less successful impact King Frederick had on his kingdom, however, came in 1777, towards the end of his reign.

Frederick reportedly became dismayed that many of his subjects were now coffee drinkers and Germany's local beer producers were suffering as a result. Coffee houses were now taking business away from inns and drinking halls across the Prussian kingdom, and fearing the tax duties that he and his government would lose from a drop in alcohol sales, Frederick decided to take decisive action.

First, in 1777, he published an official royal manifesto on the entire subject, hoping to dissuade the Prussian people from drinking coffee. "It is disgusting to notice the increase in the quantity of coffee used by my subjects," he wrote, "and the amount of money that goes out of the country in consequence. Everybody is using coffee. If possible, this must be prevented." The King's solution to the problem, however, was not quite what you might expect.

"My people must drink beer," Frederick continued. "His

Majesty was brought up on beer, and so were his ancestors and his officers. Many battles have been fought and won by soldiers nourished on beer, and the King does not believe that coffee-drinking soldiers can be depended upon to endure hardship or to beat his enemies in case of the occurrence of another war."

Next, he decreed that all coffee producers in Prussia be officially licensed by the government, but then, to control consumption of the drink, he turned down most coffee houses' license applications, permitting only those operated by friends and associates of his court. Finally, in 1781, he began employing teams of soldiers who had been injured (and therefore could no longer perform front-line military duty) to instead wander the streets of his kingdom, smelling the air for signs of illegally roasted coffee. Within a few years, Frederick was effectively running a monopoly on Prussia's coffee trade and continued to do so for the remainder of his reign.

As for Frederick himself? He reportedly loved coffee. According to royal records, he began each day by waking before dawn and drinking half a dozen cups of coffee flavored with peppercorns and mustard.

CHAPTER 53

GHOST WRITER

If you've heard of the English writer and wit Dr. Samuel Johnson, it's probably thanks to his dictionary. Johnson was essentially England's Noah Webster; he spent more than a decade of his life compiling a monumental *Dictionary of the English Language*, published in 1757. Johnson's Dictionary remained the standard, go-to dictionary of British English for the next 150 years until the very first volumes of the *Oxford English Dictionary* began to appear in the early 1900s.

As well as his work as a lexicographer, however, Johnson was also an author, diarist, critic, poet, playwright, and, for a brief time in 1762, at least, a paranormal investigator.

This particular story begins in the early 1760s when a young couple named William and Fanny Kent began renting a room from a local landlord named Richard Parsons on Cock Lane in central London. Soon after the Kent's moved in, Richard's daughter, Betty, reported hearing strange scratching and tapping sounds all around the house. After a time, she eventually claimed to have seen a ghost manifest itself in her bedroom.

Word of the supposed haunting quickly spread across the city, and it soon came to light that William Kent was not only a widower but that his new wife Fanny was his deceased wife's sister, Elizabeth. Given the laws of the day, such an arrangement was not considered legal, and Richard became convinced that the ghost must be Elizabeth's. As a result, Richard blamed William's unlawful marriage for all of the strange occurrences in his home and evicted the Kent's.

Soon afterward, the noises stopped—but when Fanny suddenly died just a few weeks later, Richard reported that they immediately resumed. Believing that it was her ghost who was now haunting his home, a series of séances were held at the Cock Lane house to get to the bottom of the mystery. Reportedly, it was through these spiritual meetings that the ghost was indeed revealed to be Fanny's, and that William Kent had poisoned her.

By now, stories of the Cock Lane Ghost were the talk of London. With a potential murder charge now mooted, the authorities were forced to step in and a criminal investigation was launched. As part of the inquiry, a committee was established to examine the details of the case, and, as one of the foremost enlightened men of 18th-century England, Samuel Johnson was invited along to record their findings. On February 1, 1762, Johnson and his team held one final séance at the Cock Lane house and he reported that Richard's daughter, Betty, became "disturbed by a spirit."

"While they were enquiring and deliberating," Johnson wrote of his team, "they were summoned into the girl's chamber by some ladies who were near her bed, and who had heard knocks and scratches. When the gentlemen entered, the girl declared that she felt the spirit like a mouse upon her back." When pressed further, however, Betty became uneasy, and the investigators grew suspicious. "Though the spirit was very solemnly required to manifest its existence by appearance," Johnson later recalled, "no evidence of any preternatural power was exhibited." He ultimately was led to believe that, "the child has some art of making or counterfeiting a particular noise, and that there is no agency of any higher cause."

As it happens, he was right. The investigation eventually discovered that Richard had borrowed a considerable amount of money from William Kent, which he had no means or intention of ever paying back. The two men had ultimately fallen out, whereupon Richard had concocted the ghost story in an elaborate attempt to frame William for both of his wives' deaths. The ghostly knocking sounds heard around the house had all been Betty's; she had secreted a tiny wooden board into the hemline of her nightdress, which she could then use to tap or scratch on the walls or furniture when prompted by her father. Both the Parsons, along with one of their servants and a preacher who was also in on the scam, were eventually prosecuted, with Richard receiving a two-year prison sentence.

The Cock Lane haunting had been revealed to be a scam, and Samuel Johnson's time as a ghost hunter was sadly over.

CHAPTER 54

FIRE IN THE BELLY

It was sometime in the late summer or early autumn of 79 CE that Mount Vesuvius — the enormous volcano in southern Italy, near the city of Naples, erupted with such enormous ferocity that many of the surrounding Roman towns and villages were obliterated. Most notable of all of these were the towns of Stabiae, Herculaneum, and most famous of all - Pompeii. Positioned at the southeastern base of Mount Vesuvius, Pompeii found itself in the direct line of fire from the eruption.

It was just after midday on the day of the eruption that fragments of ash, pumice stone, and other debris began raining down on the city of Pompeii, quickly covering the city in a thick layer of material more than 9ft deep. The weight of the debris caused roofs to collapse, trapping and killing many of the people sheltering inside, while vast superheated bursts of volcanic material and gas rapidly asphyxiated or burned all those not killed by falling debris. Over much of the following day, this cycle continued, until eventually some parts of the once vibrant city of Pompeii were buried under as much as 19ft of volcanic material. The city and its surroundings would remain encased in ash and rock for the next 1,700 years.

The ruins of Pompeii were discovered in the late 16th century, but work to excavate what remained of the city did not begin until 1748. Famously, the brutal but extraordinary way in which it was destroyed had preserved the city; along with around 1,500 of its inhabitants, in extraordinary condition. As a result, researchers at Pompeii have been able to uncover such tantalizing relics as Ancient Roman graffiti, electoral slogans, and political propaganda, "beware of the dog" signs, and even pornographic murals amid the city's ruins. All in all, the remains of Pompeii give us an all but unique insight into life in 1st century CE Roman Europe.

Of all the remarkable things uncovered at Pompeii, however, perhaps one of the most bizarre is what is properly known as *thermopolium* — or, in other words, an Ancient Roman takeaway shop.

The thermopolium at Pompeii, properly known as the Thermopolium of Asellina, after the woman who is presumed to have run it, is one of the most complete and best-preserved in all Roman archeology. Built over two floors, it is believed that the ground floor of the thermopolium operated essentially as a tavern and takeaway store, given that its large, broad doorway was left open to the street. Jugs and serving dishes were found on the shop's counter, as well as a kettle filled with water, and a series of holes were set deep into the countertop for holding jars containing food, wine, and perhaps snacks like nuts and dried fruits.

The lower floor of Asellina's shop was presumably used by customers for eating, drinking, and purchasing food to take away with them. The upper floor, however, seems likely to have had a somewhat different purpose.

169

Upstairs at the thermopolium are a series of guest rooms, which have led some researchers to believe the business operated as a tavern, with guests offered a hot meal and a bed for the evening. Others, however, believe that it likely operated as a brothel, and that the names recorded on the walls and posters in and around the premises were not those of the barmaids or serving girls but perhaps of sex workers who operated there. Whether the thermopolium indeed had a less wholesome purpose other than serving hot food will likely never be known for sure; however, its use as a handy takeaway for the people of Pompeii is assured.

CHAPTER 55

JAR OF FARTS

As the Black Plague swept across Europe in the 14th and 15th century, claiming the lives of perhaps as much as one third of the entire continent's population, then desperate people began turning to all kinds of madcap treatments and cures as a means of escaping the infection.

Among the seemingly endless list of supposed cures touted at the time were doses of undiluted vinegar or rotten treacle (which were perhaps meant to act as a purgative); taking low doses of toxic minerals like arsenic and mercury; avoiding bathing in clean water (which was believed to weaken the heart) and instead bathing in sewer water; whipping or self-flagellation (as ill-health was seen as a curse from God that required penance); burning off a bubonic fever by sitting as close to a fire as could be tolerated; strapping chicken carcasses to infected areas of the body (which was believed to draw the infection out into the bird); and even rubbing chopped onions, snake entrails, or pigeon guts onto an infected person's body.

If none of these take your fancy, of course, there's always the considerably more pleasant use of posies of fragrant flowers and herbs, often including cloves and rose petals, known as nosegays, which were worn around the neck or in front of the fact to ward off infection. Long before medical science found out the true cause of the disease, many Tudor English physicians (like those long before them) believed that bad smells and musty air must doubtless be the cause of infection and ill health. So they reasoned that breathing through more pleasant and fragrant material was a surefire way of protecting oneself from diseases.

As misguided as all of these cures were, however, smelling a posy of flower or ingesting treacle is a lot more pleasant than a cure that the physicians of London came up with when the city was struck by a further of the outbreak plague in the 17th century.

More than 200 years after the first outbreak in the medieval era, cases of the bubonic plague began to reappear in London and across England in the mid-1500s. By the turn of the century, the situation had worsened to such an extent that the city was forced to essentially go into lockdown, closing many public areas and businesses to stem the steady flow of infections through the population. Famously, it was this resurgence of the plague that forced the closure of Shakespeare's beloved Globe Theatre in 1603.

With the precise cause of the plague still unknown to physicians at the time, yet with many still believing it to be due to inhaling fetid air, doctors across London fell back on old preventative methods and quack cures to attempt to stop the disease. But some, now aware that the earlier posies and nosegays had provided little real protection from the infection, came to a contrary conclusion. If pleasant smells had not held the plague at bay, they reasoned, then perhaps the opposite was true: If a patient could dilute the foul air of the plague with an equally unpleasant aroma, perhaps that would counter the disease's course? It seemed like a perfectly sound idea at the time; and, for that matter, a perfectly simple theory to test, given that everybody has a source of foul-smelling air attached to their person. Put another way: yes, the plague doctors of 17th-century England really did encourage people to smell their own farts!

They went even further than that. Believing that foul air could drive out a foul infection, the doctors encouraged Londoners to break wind into glass bottles and jars, which they could then keep at home or on their person. As soon as they felt unwell, or believed themselves to have become infected with the plague, the doctors proscribed a quick whiff from the patient's jar of farts as a means of boosting their immunity and seeing off the disease.

Needless to say, the theory did not work. The plague continued to ravage London for another 50 years, until ironically the Great Fire of 1666 helped stem the flow of infections across the city once and for all.

CHAPTER 56

CRAZY FACTS 7

1. The tin can was patented in 1810. The tin can opener wasn't invented for another 48 years.

2. When Henry I of England died in 1135, his entrails were removed and buried in Rouen in France. The rest of his body was buried in England.

3. Of the 118 elements on the periodic table, only two are liquid at standard room temperature: mercury and bromine.

4. In 2010, a 2,400-year-old pot of soup was discovered by archeologists in Xi'an, China.

5. On average, the smallest bone in the human body — the stapes, in the inner ear — is 94 times smaller than the largest bone, the femur.

6. Buzz Aldrin claimed $33 in business expenses for his travel from Houston to the moon and back again.

7. The mortar connecting the stones of the Great Wall of China was made from rice.

8. Golf balls were originally made of wood.

9. The majority of the London Underground rail network is actually above ground.

10. On April 28, 1930, BBC radio cut to its regular evening news bulletin at 8:45 p.m., only for the announcer to state, "There is no news." Nothing of any newsworthiness had been reported that day, so the BBC played 15 minutes of piano music instead.

11. Keas, a type of parrot native to New Zealand, have been filmed deliberately using twigs to set off stoat and rat traps. Scientists eventually concluded that the birds do so just because they like the sound the traps make when they close.

12. Queen Anne was so swollen when she died in 1714 that she had to be buried in a square coffin.

13. It is believed as many as one million dogs in the United States are currently listed as the primary beneficiary of their owners' wills.

14. The most frequently encountered number in written English is one. The second is two, but the third is zero.

15. Marie Curie was the first woman to win a Nobel Prize; the first person to win the Nobel Prize twice; and the only person in history to win a Nobel Prize in two different scientific fields. She won the 1903 prize for physics and the 1911 prize for chemistry.

CHAPTER 57

DOCUMENTARY EVIDENCE

There's an old notion that Geoffrey Chaucer, author of the *Canterbury Tales* collection of stories, is the inspiration for April Fool's Day. According to the theory, in the *Nun's Priest's Tale*, the vainglorious cockerel Chauntecleer explains that he was tricked by a sly fox, *"Syn March bigan thritty dayes and two"* —which some readers take to mean March 32nd (i.e. April 1). The tricking of Chaucer's cockerel, ultimately, is said to have inspired a day on which it's perfectly acceptable to pull pranks and practical jokes.

It's a nice theory, certainly, but unfortunately, it seems untrue. April Fool's Day appears to be a French invention, developing out of an old tradition of pranking a suitably gullible person on the first of the month, and making them a *"poisson d'avril"* —an "April fish." Where this tradition derives from is unclear, but since the 1500's at least, April 1 has been established as a prime opportunity to tease people and pull off ludicrous pranks.

Nowadays, April Fool's Day is so well established that even newspaper headlines, broadcasters, and countless websites and online services all like to get in on the joke, and few have done so as successfully as Britain's national broadcaster, the BBC.

The BBC has pulled numerous April Fool's Day pranks on the unsuspecting British people over the years, including a memorable joke in 2008 in which they broadcast a news report about a colony of flying penguins discovered in the Amazon rainforest. To accompany the report, *Monty Python* actor Terry Jones was filmed first walking with penguins in Antarctica and then tracking their migratory flight path all the way to South America. Several years earlier, in 1989, the BBC's flagship sports program *Grandstand*, which was broadcast live every Saturday morning and reported the day's sports results as they came in, likewise pulled an April Fool's Day prank. They had a fight appear to break out among the program's reporters, live on air, right behind the show's presenter, Des Lynam. (The fisticuffs were only revealed to have been a prank several hours later when the program went off air.) And in 1976, the legendary BBC broadcaster and astronomer Sir Patrick Moore was heard announcing live on BBC radio, to a dumbfounded audience of millions of listeners, that due to a unique planetary alignment between Jupiter and Pluto that day, an upward gravitational pull would be created that would temporarily make everyone on early several pounds lighter, at precisely 9:47 a.m. Despite many listeners contacting the BBC to report that they indeed felt the effects of the gravitational pull, the entire story was later revealed to be a hoax.

Of all the BBC's pranks, however, perhaps the most famous was back in 1957.

Panorama is the name of one of the BBC's flagship news and current affairs programs; first broadcast in the UK in 1953, it is

177

today the longest-running news program in the world. Considered one of the most authoritative and respected news programs, each week Panorama highlights and reports on a single particularly newsworthy story, and on April 1, 1957, it broadcast a fascinating expose about spaghetti.

Swiss "spaghetti farmers," the program explained, had successfully eradicated the "spaghetti weevil" from their plantations that year and were expecting a bumper crop of pasta. Alongside the report, Panorama broadcast footage purporting to show Swiss men and women collecting strands of spaghetti from the branches of trees and shrubs in an enormous spaghetti-tree grove. The audience watching at home were totally enthralled.

Needless to say, spaghetti was still quite an exotic food in 1950s post-war Britain, so few people watching the report would have had much idea of its true origins. As a result, having such an authoritative program, presented by an authoritative journalist, the legendary BBC journalist and political reporter Richard Dimbleby, report such "news" caught many people off guard. Even after it had been revealed as a hoax, the report continued to sucker people in, while some even contacted the BBC to ask where they could get hold of a spaghetti tree, so that they could grow their own pasta in their gardens at home. Perhaps for good reason, CNN later called Panorama's spaghetti story, "the biggest hoax that any reputable news establishment ever pulled."

CHAPTER 58

CARRYING THE SPEAR

Long before the actual migratory behavior of birds and animals was known, precisely where seasonal animals went to during the winter or summer months, was a longstanding puzzle.

Unable to comprehend any other explanation, Aristotle believed that migratory animals simply morphed into one another, like a caterpillar turning into a butterfly. Another theory, proposed by Harvard vice president Charles Morton in the 17th century, claimed that birds flew ever higher as the months went by and spent the winter perched on the Moon. And even as recently as the 19th century, Victorian folklore would have you believe that swallows slept at the bottom of fishponds during the winter but hatching reinvigorated them in the spring.

As madcap as these theories might sound today, in Aristotle's era (when the true geography of the world was still relatively unknown) or the Victorian era (when the stamina and robustness of even tiny songbirds were wholly underestimated) explanations like these would have been relatively sensible. But our understanding of the natural world soon began to change thanks to a truly amazing discovering.

In 1822, a hunter in the town of Klütz, in Western Pomerania, Germany, shot down a white stork that he spotted flying past the town. As the stork tumbled to the ground, the man noticed that it was carrying with it an extraordinary bit of baggage: a 3ft-long arrow-tipped spear, which had been driven up through the bird's breast and out of the side of its neck, just below its face. Miraculously, the spear had missed the bird's vertebrae and major blood vessels, and as a result, it had survived its encounter. The stork's body was collected for scientific research, taxidermied (with the spear still in place), and put on display in the Zoological Collection of Germany's University of Rostock, where it remains to this day.

Discovering a bird that had survived such a devastating injury would be impressive enough, but it turned out that the spear impaled through the stork's body was made of African blackwood. This single stork, ultimately, could only have been impaled by such a weapon more than 2,000 miles away in Africa. This could not have occurred anywhere in Europe.

The discovery of the Klütz stock, known in German as the *pfeilstorch*, or "arrow stork", began to reshape how 19th century naturalists thought of the natural world. The birds seen in Europe in the summer clearly did not hibernate or morph into another species but instead journeyed much further than anyone could ever have anticipated, in search of better feeding grounds, nesting grounds, or opportunities to mate. A new theory of natural migration began to develop, and as the decades went by, the incontrovertible proof the *pfeilstorch* provided scientists helped them account for the annual movements of countless birds, fish, insects, and other animals.

Incredibly, in that time, another two dozen *pfeilstorchen*, each impaled on all manner of different African weaponry, were discovered across Europe, proving without a doubt that zoologists' newly emerging theories were indeed correct. The natural world, it seems, was hardier than had previously been thought, not only in surviving such a terrible injury but in being able to travel thousands of miles around the globe every single year.

CHAPTER 59

DEADHEADED

When the Vikings invaders first began arriving on the coastlines of central and western Europe, few people had seen anything more frightening. Beginning in the mid-8th century, and enduring for several hundred more years, bands of violent and bloodthirsty Norsemen ransacked their way across northern and eastern England, Scotland, Ireland, France, and other parts of mainland Europe. They burned villages, churches, and monuments to the ground, murdered anyone who crossed their path, and took whatever treasures they came across as their own. "Never before has such terror appeared in Britain as we have now suffered from a pagan race," wrote an English clergyman in York after one of the earliest raids on the region in 793 CE. "The heathens poured out the blood of saints around the altar, and trampled on the bodies of saints in the temple of God like dung in the streets."

The Vikings' violent reputation might be somewhat exaggerated according to some modern historians, who point to their extraordinarily advanced culture, literature, language, and knowledge of navigation and astronomy that all developed alongside the "raping and pillaging" with which the Vikings have become eternally associated. But as unwarranted as their reputation as violent invaders may be, the Vikings were no less successful in launching their raids on the coasts of Europe, and by the end of the 9th century, the Vikings had taken over vast swathes of territory across England, Ireland, mainland Europe, and, following a lengthy and bloody conquest in the mid-800s CE, much of northern Scotland.

One of the first Viking earls to take power over the Norse lands in Scotland is as remembered today for his violence as he was for the bizarre comeuppance that eventually caused his downfall.

Sigurd Eysteinsson, known as "Sigurd the Mighty," was made the second Viking Earl of Orkney sometime around 875 CE. Orkney, the sprawling archipelago of islands off the far northeast tip of Scotland, had first fallen under Viking control (alongside the nearby Shetland Islands) in the late 700s, when an influx of Norwegian settlers began using the islands as a base from which to operate their raids on the Scottish mainland. By the mid-800s, the islands were all incorporated into a single Viking earldom, answerable to the King of Norway, and Sigurd was given control over the region by his brother, the Norwegian Earl Rognvald Eysteinsson. Sigurd took to his newfound role with gusto, and once established on Orkney, quickly began expanding Viking rule in the area. The Viking Conquest, as it became known, pushed south from Orkney into Scotland's Caithness peninsula, as Sigurd ruthlessly stole territory from the local Celtic population. Finally, however, in 892 CE Sigurd came up against some resistance.

A local Celtic chieftain known as Mael Brigte the bucktoothed, leader of Moray, raised an army to fight back against Sigurd's conquest of the area. Mael challenged Sigurd to a simple battle, of equal strength, 40 men on either side, with the victor either taking or retaining control of Mael's kingdom. Sigurd accepted Mael's invitation, yet treacherously turned up to the battle with twice the agreed number of men. Sigurd's 80 Viking soldiers quickly defeated Mael's band of Celtic fighters, and with his victory assured, Sigurd personally sought out Mael on the battlefield and decapitated him. He then picked up Mael's head and tied it to his horse's saddle, to carry it back to Orkney as proof of his uncompromising leadership and victory in battle. Enroute back home, however, Sigurd began to take ill.

On the long journey back north, the "bucktooth" in Mael's mouth that had given him his less than flattering nickname began to chafe and eventually cut Sigurd's leg. The wound quickly became infected, and long before he arrived back in Orkney, he died as a result of the injury. Sigurd's treachery on the battlefield, it seemed, had ultimately proved his undoing.

CHAPTER 60

STRIKE ONE

The very first labor strike in American history occurred right back at the very founding of what is now the United States. In 1619, the burgeoning colony of Virginia held its first elections, but despite having been living and working in Jamestown for over a decade, a vast number of Dutch and Polish craftsmen were not permitted to vote. The reason given was that they were not of English descent. In response, the craftsmen, who produced tar, pitch, turpentine, and other similar products that were needed in building ships, went on strike. The craftsmen's work was considered so important, and there were so few other people in Jamestown who could carry out the work in their place, that the Virginia Company leaders were compelled to change their minds and awarded the continental workers full voting rights.

America's first strike, then, occurred more than four centuries ago. The very first strike in recorded history, however, took place more than three *millennia* ago.

Sometime around 1157 BCE, the pharaoh Ramses III was overseeing the construction of some of the tombs, catacombs, and pyramids that form what is known today as the Valley of the Kings. Slaves and stonemasons were used to construct these enormous structures, but their decoration was left to teams of professional and highly-skilled craftsmen and artisans, whom the pharaoh called in to work on the tombs in secret. These artisans were responsible for the elaborately painted interiors still visible in many of the tombs to this day, with frescos and murals covering all the walls from floor to ceiling.

But at one of these locations, a village named Deir el Medina, near Thebes on the west bank of the river Nile, the workers under Pharaoh Ramses' employ began to become restless. A papyrus scroll dating from the time records that after 18 days of near-constant working, the workers at the Royal Necropolis in Deir el Medina had still not received any food rations. They were essentially being left to feed and fend for themselves, all while working nonstop on the Pharaoh's tombs. Eventually, the situation became so dire—and the workforce became so famished, that the builders and craftsmen at Deir el Medina decided to stage a sit-down strike.

On day ten of the "second month of winter" in the 29th year of Ramses' reign, the papyrus explains, the workers walked into the mortuary that they were currently working on at Deir el Medina. There, they set down their tools and ceased working, in protest over the dire conditions the Pharaoh was expecting them to work under. "The prospect of hunger and thirst has driven us to this," they are recorded as saying. "There is no clothing, there is no ointment, there is no fish, there are no vegetables."

"We are hungry," the workers' protest continued, "and 18

days have already elapsed in this month" without any rations being forthcoming. "We have matters with the pharaoh."

After several days, a local statesman, equivalent to a chief of police, was called in to speak with the strikers and on hearing their plight agreed that the situation was untenable. Together, they marched on the pharaoh's palace, with their wives and children in tow, and brought their protest right to the Pharaoh's court in Thebes.

In an attempt to see off the uprising, the workers were initially offered half a sack of barley each, and platters of rich pastries were handed out among the crowd. These arrangements quelled the protest for a day or two, but with still no resolution in sight, the strike continued the following morning.

How the strike was eventually resolved has sadly not been recorded in the original documents, as the attention of the Pharaoh and his court eventually turned to organizing lavish celebrations to mark the 30th anniversary of Ramses III's ascent to power. We can presume, however, that an agreement was eventually struck with the striking workers, as proved by the decoration of the tombs of Deir el Medina.

CHAPTER 61

WHATEVER FLOATS YOUR BOAT

In 2016, an ecological organization based in the UK called the Natural Environment Research Council invited its members and the British public at large to name the latest acquisition to its fleet of research vessels: a £200 million ($330 million) state-of-the-art polar research ship.

The vessel, which was to be built in Liverpool, was essentially a floating laboratory, which the NERC would use in its ongoing work studying the effects of climate change in the polar regions. Filled with enthusiasm for what this ship would bring to their work, the Council eagerly announced their #NameOurShip campaign on social media and handed the task of naming the vessel over to the public. As often is the case in these situations, however, the public were perhaps not the best people to ask...

Shortly after the campaign was launched, a BBC journalist named James Hand, who was working for a radio station in Britain's Channel Islands, jokingly commented that the vessel should be named "Boaty McBoatface", a reference to a popular internet meme featuring an owl at a British zoo, which the zoo's visitors had decided to christen "Hooty

McOwlface." Hand's suggestion, however, proved instantly popular with the station's listeners, and when news of its popularity was announced online, "Boaty McBoatface" took on a life of its own.

Likely much to the NERC's chagrin, "Boaty McBoatface" quickly began to garner the most votes in their #NameOurShip poll, and as voting came to a close, "Boaty McBoatface" remained the front runner in the campaign. Finally, the public had spoken: The votes were counted and the Council's new and much-publicized £200 million research vessel was, it seems, to be called the RSS *Boaty McBoatface*.

As much as the public might have taken to the idea, however, calling a hugely important research vessel "Boaty McBoatface" is not such a good idea. As a result, the NERC decided to accept the results of the poll but take matters into their own hands.

Instead of "Boaty McBoatface," the Council decided to go with the second most popular name in the public poll, and name their ship in honor of the legendary broadcaster and naturalist, Sir David Attenborough. In a fitting tribute, the NERC's decision was announced just days before Sir David's 90th birthday.

"I am truly honored by this naming decision, and hope that everyone who suggested a name will feel just as inspired to follow the ship's progress as it explores our polar regions," Sir David said at the time. "I have been privileged to explore the world's deepest oceans alongside amazing teams of researchers, and with this new polar research ship they will be able to go further and discover more than ever before."

For their part, however, the NERC were fully aware that they couldn't just ignore the public's voice completely.

"The NERC Name Our Ship campaign has engaged the public with the ship's mission on a huge scale," they commented at the time, "and we are very grateful for the support and enthusiasm shown by the public in contributing to naming for our new research vessel the RSS Sir David Attenborough."

"We are also very happy," they went on, "to recognize the overall popular choice, through naming one of the ship's robotic vehicles *Boaty McBoatface*."

The RRS *Sir David Attenborough*, as it was ultimately known, was launched three years later in 2019. On board was *Boaty McBoatface*, a specialized submarine-like autonomous underwater submersible, used to conduct research and experiment in arctic waters. The two vessels continue to monitor the polar landscape under the NERC's guidance to this day.

CHAPTER 62

THE BIG CHEESE

Queen Victoria married her sweetheart, the German Prince Albert of Saxe-Coburg and Gotha, in a lavish ceremony at the Chapel Royal in St. James' Palace, London, on February 10, 1840. Understandably, the wedding was an enormous affair, and one of the most anticipated events of its day. Victoria was an immensely popular monarch among the British people, and with interest and respect for the royal family and her empire at an all-time high in the 19th century, all of England rallied behind the young queen. Thousands of well-wishers lined the streets of London, and cards, gifts, and tributes were sent to the Queen and her new consort from all corners of the United Kingdom. And, as a true sign of just how popular and respected Queen Victoria was, her wedding proved hugely influential too: She bucked the trend at the time for wearing pastel-shaded wedding gowns, and instead wore a simple, bright white wedding dress. White wedding dresses have remained the tradition for brides' first marriages ever since.

Among all of the celebrations and gifts sent to Queen Victoria on her wedding day, however, perhaps one of the most remarkable was that which a group of dairy farmers took it upon themselves to produce for her in the far southwest corner of England.

When it became known that the Queen was set to marry, an alliance of farmers from two villages, East and West Pennard, in the county of Somerset, decided to combine forces and produce for her the world's largest block of cheddar cheese. In June 1839, as many as 750 dairy cows were milked, by a team of 50 local milkmaids, and their milk used to make an enormous 1,250lb cheddar, set into a 9ft-wide octagonal mahogany mold. As the cheese hardened and matured, to ensure that it was truly fit for a queen to consume, it was stamped and embossed with the royal coat of arms.

By Queen Victoria's wedding day the following year, the cheese had matured enough to be transported to London and was presented to her royal highness on February 10, 1840, in suitably ostentatious fashion. Not only was she to be given the world's biggest cheddar cheese, but a duo of local musicians had written a song about the farmers' efforts, which was performed for the Queen as the cheese was unveiled at the palace.

The Queen herself, it seems, much appreciated the Pennard farmers' efforts, but on tasting a sliver of the cheese reportedly announced that she preferred a cheddar with a more mature flavor, and declined to eat any more. That, however, left her at something of a loss over what best to do with a 9ft octagon of cheddar cheese that she didn't particularly want to eat.

Eventually, it was decided that the record-breaking cheese should be sent on a tour of Queen Victoria's kingdom, and so the enormous cheddar was packed up once more and taken off around the UK to be displayed at various locations. Anyone who wished to come and take a look at the world's largest block of cheese was required to purchase a ticket, with the money raised by the ticket sales later donated to various good causes in the Queen's name. The cheese, it seems, proved immensely popular with the British public who (perhaps for good reason) had never seen anything quite like it before.

Once the tour was over, arrangements began to be made to return once more the cheese to its rightful owner, but Queen Victoria, understandably, wasn't too keen to have it back. Instead, it was sent back to Somerset, where its producers argued over what best to do with the now considerably old and rather dry and damaged block of cheese.

As a result, despite once being fit for royalty, the world's largest cheddar met an ignominious end: It was simply broken up and fed to the farmers' pigs.

CHAPTER 63

BATTLE OF BRITAIN

Great Britain famously defended itself so pugnaciously during World War Two that no mainland British soil was occupied by Germany.

It's often said that the only British-owned territory on the face of the globe that *did* fall under Nazi occupation was the Channel Islands, a tiny archipelago off the northwest coast of France. The islands remained under German rule from their capture on June 30, 1940, until their liberation on May 9, 1945.

Britain has fared so well during the countless conflicts and wars in which it has been involved that the last time there was an invasion of the British mainland was in 1797. And to say it ended shambolically is something of an understatement.

At that time, England was embroiled in a series of bitter cross-European conflicts that became known as the War of the First Coalition. The war simmered for around five years, during which time a huge number of European powers, including Britain, Spain, the Netherlands, the Habsburg Empire, the Holy Roman Empire, and the city-states of Naples and Venice, fought among one another and against Revolutionary France.

The long-time hostility between France and England, meanwhile, only became even more exacerbated by the conflict, and when France sided with Ireland (which was at that time under British rule), a French general named Lazare Hoche devised a complex three-pronged attack on Britain aimed at weakening the British armed forces, diminishing its rule in Ireland, and bolstering the Irish independence movement.

Hoche's tactics were as follows. Two French parties of around 1,500 troops would land in mainland England: one near Newcastle on England's northeast coast, the other on the west coast of Wales. These were meant merely as diversionary invasions, splitting the UK's troops in two and forcing the UK to withdraw some of its forces from Ireland to bolster those at home on the British mainland. Meanwhile, a third much larger body of 15,000 French troops would land at Bantry Bay in County Cork in southern Ireland. There, with the aid of the Society of United Irishmen, they would take on the remaining British troops, and boost the Irish republican and revolutionary movements.

With Hoche's maneuvers in place, the forces set sail in December 1796. On paper, it seemed like the perfect ploy. What Hoche had not factored into his plans, however, was the weather in the English Channel in the depths of a northern European winter.

The 15,000 troops due to land at Bantry Bay found the Irish coast utterly without safe harbor in the fierce winter weather. Unable to land a single ship, the French fleet bound for Ireland was forced to retreat back to France. The ships bound for Newcastle likewise met trouble in the middle of the North Sea, and the poor weather conditions—coupled with outbreaks of mutiny and poor discipline among the French recruits, forced the Newcastle-bound troops to abandon their aims and they too returned to France. The four ships bound for Wales, however, soldiered on. Finding the weather in the relatively more sheltered Irish Sea more bearable, under cover of darkness on the night of 22 February, 1,400 French soldiers—blissfully unaware that the rest of Hoche's plans had failed, landed on the beach at Carregwastad Head, near the town of Fishguard, in Pembrokeshire, Wales. By 2 a.m. the following morning, they had unloaded some 47 barrels of gunpowder, 50 tons of gun cartridges and grenades, and 2,000 weapons. Now appropriately well-armed, the French forces began to move inland along the Llanwnda Peninsula, occupying several homesteads and farm buildings on the way, aiming to secure a high vantage point from which to defend the surrounding area. The invasion had officially begun, but almost as soon as it had, disaster struck.

Only around 600 of the 1,400 French troops who landed at Fishguard were regular troops in the French army, as much of the French forces were at that time embroiled in Napoleon's ill-fated attempt to conquer Italy. The remaining 800 invaders were a ragtag bunch of irregulars, including convicts, deserters, and anti-republican prisoners who had been drafted into the French forces to bolster their numbers. Almost as soon as they arrived in Wales, many of these irregulars deserted the French cause and fled into the Welsh countryside. The situation worsened when dozens of the French troops happened to find that many of the buildings in the area contained huge quantities of fine Portuguese wine; a shipwreck several weeks earlier had left hundreds of wine bottles washed up on the Fishguard coast, and the locals had been keen to make the most of the unexpected bounty. As a result, by the end of the second day of the invasion, many of the French forces were either missing or drunk.

In response to the invasion, British forces in the area were roused and placed under the command of Lord Cawdor, a captain in the local Pembroke Yeomanry Cavalry. A hastily-assembled militia of around 500 local Welsh reservists, sailors, and civilians—many armed with pokers, mallets, pans, and whatever else they could lay their hands on, also arrived on the scene to attempt to hold back the invasion.

Several brief clashes ensued across the region, but the French forces were quickly repelled. With discipline and morale now quickly failing among the French troops, the arrival of a much more impressive British counterforce than they were expecting proved the final straw. Lord Cawdor issued the French troops an ultimatum to either surrender or face attack, and at 2 p.m. on February 24, the French forces laid down their weapons.

After just 48 hours, the so-called Battle of Fishguard, the last mainland invasion of British soil, was over.

CHAPTER 64

CRAZY FACTS 8

1. Dolphins hear through their jawbones.

2. Charles Dickens invented the word *boredom*.

3. The world's largest collection of plant seeds is housed in an underground vault on the Arctic island of Svalbard. The collection is intended to be used only in the event of an apocalyptic collapse in the Earth's biodiversity.

4. LEGO manufactures more tires per year than any automobile company.

5. The world's biggest-selling chocolate shop is the duty-free store in Brussels Airport.

6. Scotland's Loch Ness contains more water than all the lakes in the rest of Great Britain combined.

7. Florence Nightingale had a pet owl called Athena.

8. Some astronomers believe that the Star of Jerusalem the Three Wise Men followed to Jesus' birth was probably the planet Jupiter.

9. Hawaiian pizza, topped with ham and pineapple, was invented in Canada.

10. *Star Trek* creator Gene Roddenberry was so opposed to a captain in the series being bald, that when Sir Patrick Stewart auditioned for *The Next Generation*, he was made to wear a wig.

11. As well as being associated with love and romance, St Valentine is also the patron saint of epilepsy, beekeepers, and the plague.

12. The world's smallest insect is about the same size as the world's largest bacteria.

13. Some canals in England have special lanes for ducks to walk down.

14. America spent more money landscaping Central Park than it did in the Alaska Purchase.

15. In 1999, an Australian man won a new car on a lottery scratch card. While being interviewed about his win for local television, he bought another ticket to reenact his victory — and won $250,000.

CONCLUSION

With that, our final crazy stories are complete. And what a journey it was.

We now know how an impaled stork helped in our understanding of the natural world, and how you might be able to fool your doctor into believing you've given birth to a litter of rabbits. We also know how much Bach liked coffee, and how much Frederick the Great hated coffee. We know why the MGM lion doesn't roar before *Ben-Hur*, why there's never been a movie of *The Mousetrap*, and why Sir Alec Guinness is only in the second *Star Wars* film for a matter of seconds (despite pocketing nearly half a million dollars for his performance).

We know how important pee was to the Ancient Romans, and how important farts were to 17th-century plague-fearing Londoners. We know how lucky we are to have *The Catcher in the Rye* on our bookshelves, how clever octopuses are, how good Henry VIII was at wresting, and how not to test a homemade parachute. We know why the Queen of England has a gold disk, how Thomas Jefferson inspired a 19th-century catchphrase, and why turning down President John Quincy Adams' invitation to row him across the Potomac river with no clothes on was probably a good move. And now, we also know that if you're going to spend $330 million on a scientific polar research vessel, you *probably* shouldn't ask the British public to help name it.

These have all been some of the craziest, weirdest, wackiest, and most awesome stories we could ever have told you. And what makes it even more awesome, is that there are a lot more crazy stories out there to tell!

Made in the USA
Middletown, DE
19 December 2020

29361224R00116